THE HANDBOOK OF
STUDENT SKILLS

For John and Michael

THE HANDBOOK OF STUDENT SKILLS

Neil Burdess

Prentice Hall

New York London Toronto Sydney Tokyo Singapore

Acquisitions Editor: Michael Page
Production Editor: Fiona Marcar
Cover design: Kim Webber.
Cartoonist: B. Akhurst, Oakwood Art, Burradoo, NSW.
Typesetter: Keyboard Wizards, Harbord, NSW.

Printed in Australia by Impact Printing, Brunswick, VIC.

2 3 4 5 95 94 93 92 91

ISBN 0 7248 1086 2

National Library of Australia
Cataloguing-in-Publication Data

Burdess, Neil.
    The handbook of student skills.

    Bibliography.
    Includes index.
    ISBN 0 7248 1086 2.

    1. Study, Method of. I. Title.

378.170281

Prentice Hall, Inc., *Englewood Cliffs, New Jersey*
Prentice Hall Canada, Inc., *Toronto*
Prentice Hall Hispanoamericana, SA, *Mexico*
Prentice Hall of India Private Ltd, *New Delhi*
Prentice Hall International, Inc., *London*
Prentice Hall of Japan, Inc., *Tokyo*
Prentice Hall of Southeast Asia Pty Ltd, *Singapore*
Editora Prentice Hall do Brasil Ltda, *Rio de Janeiro*

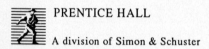 PRENTICE HALL

A division of Simon & Schuster

Contents

2 Library skills 60

1

Study skills

Introduction

Social science and humanities staff in colleges and universities base their professional relationship with their students on two basic principles: (1) that students are adults who have a right and responsibility to manage their own lives; and (2) that students have the intelligence, experience and motivation to learn with the minimum amount of formal teaching. The practical consequences of these principles are that, in order to be a successful student, you need: (1) time-management skills so that you can balance the time you spend on your academic and non-academic activities; and (2) learning skills so that you can get the most out of the time you spend on your academic work. The basic aim of this chapter is to help you develop these skills.

Time management

Tertiary students vary enormously in their personal circumstances — in age, educational background, type of accommodation, mode of study, financial support, and so on. But whatever your particular situation, there are **four major calls on your time**: personal, economic, social, and academic (Scharf with Hait 1985, p. 10). It is the relative importance of each that varies with your particular circumstances. Personal activities include washing, dressing and eating, and the very time-consuming household chores of shopping, cooking and cleaning. Economic activities are those concerned with acquiring, organising and spending money. (The first is most difficult; the last is least difficult!) Social activities include everything from going to a student union disco to visiting a sick grandmother. Academic activities include class work, when you attend lectures, tutorials, and seminars; and private study, when you prepare for your class work and write your assignments.

How effectively you manage your time depends partly on how well you plan your time, and partly on how well you get to know how your college or university functions. I'll look at each in turn.

Planning your time

As a tertiary student, you will have to manage your life to make sure that you **balance** your personal, economic and social activities with your academic work. Only you can say what the right balance is — it depends on your abilities, ambitions, interests and personality. As a very general guide, I suggest that if you're studying part-time, you start your degree by working for about 10 hours per week on each unit or subject; if you're a full-time student, aim to study for approximately 40 hours per week. It should take you no more than a few weeks to decide whether or not you've got the right balance between your academic and non-academic activities. If you don't take notice of your in-built balancing system, you are likely to experience what Elizabeth Hastings (1984, p. 8) calls 'contaminated time' — you don't give your full attention and energy to what you're doing, and therefore don't enjoy yourself or achieve very much. For example, you may feel uncomfortable away from your desk because you think that you should be studying; or you may feel uncomfortable at your desk because you've been studying for too long, and think that you should be doing something different.

To help you maintain a balance between your academic and non-academic activities you need to plan your time. To do this well, you need both a long-term plan for the term or semester, and a series of short-term plans for each week of the teaching period. I'll start by looking at term or semester plans.

Term or semester plans

At the start of the term or semester, the co-ordinator of each unit should hand out a program which includes the submission dates for any assignment work. In addition, your university or college handbook should include a calendar of important dates such as the start and end of each term or semester, any residential schools for off-campus students, and the exam periods. Obtain a **large year planner** — you can buy one, or some companies give them away for advertising purposes. Mark on it the important dates from each course unit handout and the university or college handbook. Also include on your year planner any other major activities with fixed dates: your team's sporting fixtures, your sister's wedding, the camping expedition you promised your son, and so on.

Before each assignment deadline you will spend a lot of time preparing the assignment. Highlight this **preparation time** on the year planner: draw an arrow starting from the day you expect to start on the assignment with the arrowhead at the day before you have to hand in the assignment. Of course, at the start of the academic year you may have little idea of exactly how much time you will spend on each assignment. However, apart from an early period when there will be very little assessment work, the chances are your preparation periods will be determined largely by the number of assignments you have to complete. Pin your year planner on the wall next to your desk, or wherever you can keep a close eye on it. Then you can see at a glance what your next commitments are — and plan accordingly.

Weekly plans

Weekly plans are essential for all students, whether full-time or part-time. If you're a full-time student, you may have only 10 or 15 hours per week of formal classes, the rest being largely 'free' time. Without a plan for the week, the days can slip by as you delay your private study, believing that you have so much time that there is no need to start studying right away. In contrast, if you're a part-time student, you may have 40 or 50 hours per week allocated to non-academic activities. Without a plan for the week, the days can slip by as these activities crowd out your academic work. Thus, whatever your circumstances, make sure that you draw up a detailed plan for each week.

At the very least, you should include the commitments listed on the year planner, your class times (if you're an on-campus student), your hours of employment (if you're a part-time student), and any other activities with specific times (e.g. when it's your turn to cook dinner for everyone in the flat; when you take your daughter to her music lesson; when you stack supermarket shelves; or when you practise with your basketball team or choir). The remaining time is potentially available for private study.

There are two basic ways of making sure that you do the necessary amount of private study during the time remaining on the weekly timetable: backward planning, and (not surprisingly) forward planning. In **backward planning** you commit yourself to a certain number of hours of private study at some time during the week. Each time you complete at least a half hour's study, you add it to your list of work done, and note how much there is still left to do. You thus plan your next study session by looking back at what you have done in previous sessions. In **forward planning** you commit yourself not only to a certain number of hours of private study, but also to study particular subjects at specified times (e.g. on Tuesdays between 8 and 9 you study sociology). Which planning method you use is up to you. The important thing is that you *plan* your week — don't just muddle along with a 'She'll be right mate' attitude.

Of course, as the Scottish poet Robbie Burns points out, 'The best laid schemes o' mice and men/Gang aft a-gley'. In other words, **even the best plans sometimes come unstuck**. If you find that you didn't do as much academic work as you had planned, try to work out the reason why. Look carefully over the previous week to see exactly how you spent your time. If you find that virtually no time can be classed as wasted time, you need to balance your academic and non-academic activities by cutting back on some of your personal, economic, or social activities. This is a choice that you are most likely to face if you're a part-time student, trying to fit studying into an already busy lifestyle. If you can't, or won't, cut back on your non-academic activities, then the only alternative is to reduce your academic workload.

However, particularly if you're a full-time student, it's much more likely that you will find that you have **wasted time** watching TV, chatting endlessly, or spending too long in bed — all popular student activities! You need to balance your academic and non-academic work by reducing the amount of time wasted on your personal and social activities. For example, if you seem to spend too long watching television, you could draw up a weekly viewing schedule of TV shows, and make sure that you watch only these. If possible, videotape them so that you can watch them at times convenient to you — and spend as little time as possible watching the ads.

Getting to know the system

So far I have concentrated on you as an individual, but you are also part of a much larger social environment — your university or college. You will make more effective use of your time if you know how your institution functions (McEvedy & Jordan 1986, Part 3). I'll illustrate the range of ways in which getting to know the system can help you organise your academic and non-academic activities.

Academic issues

All institutions publish **handbooks** which outline the units on offer, the structure of degree courses, and the various regulations relating to enrolling and withdrawing from units and courses. If you don't receive detailed information from your department, you should use the handbook to get to know the structure of your degree course. It will help you to choose the most appropriate units.

Courses vary in their degree of **flexibility**. In some, all the units may be compulsory; in others, you may be able to choose most of your units from a long list of options. Similarly, courses vary in their use of prerequisite regulations. For example, in one course Economics 1A may be a prerequisite for Economics 1B. In other words, you need to have passed Economics 1A before you can enrol for Economics 1B. In another course you may be able to enrol in Economics 1B without having passed Economics 1A. The more flexible the course, the more options you have — but the more planning you have to do yourself.

There are also regulations about **enrolling and withdrawing** from units and courses. You may find that an individual unit, or even the entire course, is not what you expected. After much cool and rational thought, you may decide to alter your original registration form. If you wish to withdraw from an individual unit, find out how, if at all, your enrolment in the unit will appear on your record of results. For example, if you withdraw after a certain date, you may be classified as having failed the unit. Similarly, find out the financial implications of withdrawing. For example, are you still eligible for a full government grant? If you are withdrawing from the entire course, can you receive a refund of enrolment fees, and any graduate tax contributions? If you also want to enrol in a new unit or course, check to see that the system allows a late enrolment. If it is a second semester unit, be clear about how your new program will affect your unit enrolments in the next academic year.

Make sure of your department's policy on the **submission of assignments**. Often, to complete a unit you have to hand in all assignments. For example, even though you have more than the pass mark from three of the four assignments, you must still submit the fourth assignment in order to pass the unit. There are also variations in departmental policy about assignment deadlines. For example, in our department, we reduce the assessed mark by 5% for every working day that the assignment is late; after 10 working days it is not marked. For off-campus students we use the postmarked date on the envelope to indicate the submission date, but it could be that in your department assignments must actually *arrive* by the due date. If you're very concerned about your assignment going missing in the mail, then you should consider registering the envelope. In any case, always keep a copy of the assignment. You can reassure yourself that the package has arrived by filling in a receipt-of-assignment form for the university or college to mail back to you.

Non-academic issues

In this section I'll show how other people working at your university or college can often help you with personal, economic or social problems. The most common **personal problems** are those concerned with illness. Find out about the student health service. It's probably convenient, understanding, and cheap: conveniently located on-campus; staffed by people who understand student pressures and problems; and likely to bulk bill, thus keeping your costs to a minimum. Illness, of course, disrupts even the best laid plans. Thus, it is useful to find out about the regulations concerning illness and assignment deadlines. Teaching staff will react sympathetically if you have been sick, but they will usually require documentary evidence of illness. Make sure that your doctor gives you a certificate which shows the period during which you have been unwell, so that you can be granted an extension to the assessment deadline. For other personal difficulties, such as fear of public speaking, sleeping problems, or an inability to organise your private study time, the best source of advice is the student counselling service. Counsellors are familiar with the range of personal problems which students often face. If they can't help you themselves they will be able to direct you to people who can.

Most institutions provide advice about **economic problems**. For example, your student union or counselling service can give you information about government grants and taxes. You can also get advice about any student concessions for such things as public transport and cinema admission. In an emergency, you may be able to get an interest-free loan from your university or college. Your campus might have an employment officer, who will help you find part-time work. Finally, check out what's available at the second-hand campus bookshop — but make doubly sure that any books you buy for a course are still prescribed texts, or at least highly recommended readings.

BALANCING THE STUDENT BUDGET

Lastly, there are a number of **social problems** that can occur. For example, you may feel that you are being subjected to sexual harassment; or you might become involved in a dispute with the owner of your flat; or you may have serious family problems; or you may get into legal difficulties. If you have any problems like these, seek assistance from the student counselling service. One of the counsellors' main jobs is to help you get through these sorts of crises. If necessary, make use of their expertise.

Although the above comments apply most obviously to on-campus students (and particularly those attending classes during the day), bear in mind that all these services are also available to off-campus students during residential schools, and that the student counsellors and student union officers can always be contacted by telephone or mail.

So far the discussion has been very broad-ranging. I have stressed the importance of time management: achieving a balance between your academic and non-academic activities; and making use of your college or university system to help you maintain this balance. Following Figure 1.1 I'll spend the rest of the chapter looking in detail at how to get the most from your academic work.

There are two types of academic work: **class work**, where you and other students meet with staff at times set by the institution; and **private study**, where you work largely as an individual at times set by yourself. The two types of academic work are closely linked, as what you do in class can greatly influence what you do in your private study, and vice versa. There are three main types of class work: lectures, tutorials and seminars. For each, I'll firstly discuss what to do in your private study to prepare for the class; then I'll look at how to participate effectively during the class; and finally I'll show you how to use your private study time to carry out a review of the class to help you learn the material.

My comments about lectures, tutorials and seminars will apply most directly to on-campus students. However, there are several reasons why off-campus students will also benefit from reading these sections. Firstly, most off-campus programs include residential schools held on-campus, which include lectures, tutorials and seminars. Secondly, 'tele-tutorials' will become increasingly common during the 1990s, linking on-campus tutors with off-campus students via a telephone (or video) link. Finally, lectures and tutorials can be a normal part of an external program: the course materials often include audio or video recordings of lectures; and

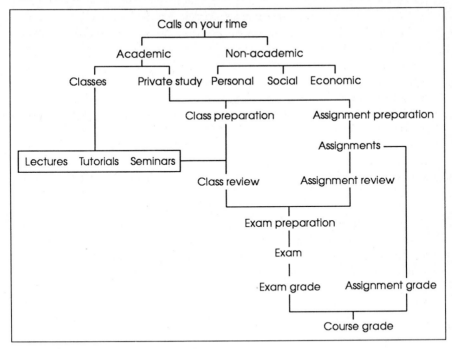

Figure 1.1 Academic work

staff encourage off-campus students to form their own tutorial groups to discuss their work.

Lectures

The traditional lecture is a one-way communication process — the lecturer speaks, and the students listen and probably take notes. Although often severely criticised as an ineffective teaching device, the lecture remains a very common teaching method in tertiary education. This is largely because a lecture is a means of mass communication — one lecturer can, if necessary, communicate with several hundred students at the same time. In a period when the number of tertiary students is growing at a faster rate than the number of tertiary teachers, it is likely that lectures will continue to be a major teaching method in colleges and universities.

There is a range of **lecturing styles**. Some lecturers see their major task to be the preparation of their lecture notes — to provide a clear, up-to-date overview of each topic, perhaps from a number of perspectives. The lecture itself is simply a method of transferring this information to the students. It is done in a straightforward, unexciting way, the primary aim being to inform rather than to excite interest. In contrast, other lecturers see their major task to be the presentation of a few key ideas in such a way as to stimulate students to find out more about the topic for themselves. These lecturers often adopt a theatrical style, the primary aim being to excite interest rather than simply to inform. In practice, most lecturers use a combination of the two styles, though probably most are on the instructional rather than the theatrical side of the range. As I'll point out later, a lecturer's style influences the sort of notes you take during the lecture.

There are a number of **criticisms of traditional lectures**. As you may have noticed already, some lecturers are rather poor communicators. This is not surprising once you realise that many lecturers are appointed more on their *research* record than their teaching abilities, and very few have had any formal instruction about how to teach. However, the criticism of lectures goes deeper than this. Critics see two fundamental problems. Firstly, the attention span of the average student is very much shorter than the 50 to 60 minutes of the average lecture. Indeed, concentration levels are very low after only 20 minutes (Gibbs, Habeshaw & Habeshaw 1987, p. 101). A second criticism relates to a student's two basic goals when attending a lecture: to *understand* and to *record* what the lecturer says. Gibbs and his colleagues suggest that these two goals are incompatible (p. 29). For example, the more carefully you listen, in an attempt to understand the lecturer, the less carefully you can record what the lecturer says.

It is in **response to these criticisms** that some lecturers use a modified version of the traditional lecture. To counteract the problem of rapidly declining student performance, some lecturers follow the advice of Graham Gibbs and his colleagues (1987), and use a variety of techniques to ensure that they talk for no more than 15 to 20 minutes without a break. For example, after 20 minutes lecturing, some lecturers call a 5-minute break to allow students to stretch, chat, or have a breath of fresh air (or tobacco smoke); others organise buzz groups of two to three students to discuss the lecture material for a few minutes; some lecturers ask you to read and make notes for 10 to 15 minutes, in preparation for the next part of the lecture; and others simply ask you to sit quietly for a minute or so and reflect on what you have just heard.

To counteract the criticism that listening and note-taking are incompatible activities, some lecturers provide their students with **lecture handouts**. For example, the university where I work is one of several in Australia with off-campus students. As they can't come to lectures, we send them study guides containing most of the points raised in the lectures. Some lecturers also make these study guides available to on-campus students. Thus, when preparing lectures, I assume that the students in the audience will have copies of the study guide. I use the lectures simply to highlight the most important points, showing visual aids to help make the points more memorable. Students can concentrate on listening and understanding and still have a comprehensive set of notes at the end of the lecture. Of course, only a minority of lecturers have the opportunity to use study guides, but all lecturers can use more limited handouts: lists of main points, important diagrams, tables, reading lists, and so on.

However, it is likely that most of your lectures will be traditional ones: the lecturer will talk without a break for 50 to 60 minutes, and will provide little in the way of lecture handouts. Consequently, I'll concentrate on how to get the most out of traditional lectures. Most importantly, you need to see your attendance at the lecture as a middle step in a **developmental sequence**: firstly, you prepare for the lecture; secondly, you attend the lecture; and, finally, you review what you have learned from the lecture. I'll look at each in turn.

Before the lecture

When you prepare for the lecture, you need to do two things. Firstly, you need to see **how this particular lecture fits into the overall structure of the unit**. During the first lecture the co-ordinator of the unit should give you a program of topics to be covered. This provides a sketch map of the intellectual path that the lecturer will take you along. It is useful to see where you have got to, how you got there, and where you will go next. This orientation process will usually take only a couple of minutes — even less when you become familiar with the structure of the unit. It is a couple of minutes well spent.

The second function of the preparation stage — to continue the above analogy — is to see what is already recorded in your guidebook, so that you spend time noting down only additional information about your latest port of call. In other words, in the lecture **take notes only about new material** — that is, points not already covered in the textbook or lecture handouts. Of course, you can make the distinction between existing and new material only if you know what's in the textbook and handouts. At this stage there is no need to do detailed reading, or any note-making. Just become familiar with the basic structure of the material. Look at the headings used by the author, as these show the major themes in the reading. For example, you could get some overall impression of the development of this chapter simply by looking at the section headings.

During the lecture

Try to **arrive early and take a seat near the front**. From here you will be able to hear better, see the board and projector screen more clearly, and have fewer distractions between yourself and the lecturer. Being there from the start of the lecture is obviously a courtesy to the lecturer, and it also means that you won't miss out on any handouts. Nor will you miss out on what is often the most valuable part of the lecture, as during the first few minutes the speaker often quickly reviews relevant arguments from previous lectures, and outlines the main objectives of the current lecture.

Psychologists refer to the processes of perception and cognition: perception is taking in information from the environment through our senses; cognition is making sense of this information. Similarly, I'll make a distinction between hearing and listening. Hearing is a physical process — taking in sound through your ears. **Listening is a mental process** — trying to make sense of this information. Listening intently for an hour or so is undoubtedly hard work, doubly so when you are also trying to take notes about what is being said.

Your **level of concentration** is affected by other events happening in the lecture hall. Lecturers themselves can often distract you with mannerisms such as tracing imaginary quotation marks in the air, or prefacing each point by saying 'You know'. Some students end up concentrating entirely on these mannerisms, counting the number of times they occur during the lecture. This is not a very productive use of time! If a lecturer is very approachable, you might be able to drop a broad hint about a distracting mannerism. Otherwise, the only advice is to learn to ignore it, or at least to become tolerant of it.

Other students in the audience are another source of distraction. If you sit near the front of the lecture theatre you cut out the potentially large number of heads between yourself and the lecturer. It's amazing just how interesting these heads can be when you begin to tire and lose concentration! Occasionally, students who lack the necessary listening skills end up completely ignoring the lecture, and spend their time chatting to each other. Don't let them waste your time as well as their own. Peer pressure can often work wonders. Usually the problem is short-lived as chatterers quickly come to realise that a caf or pub are more pleasant places to pass the time than a lecture theatre.

So what do you actually do when the lecturer is speaking? The short answer is to **listen for the main points**, and write them down. The first task is listening. Remember that listening is different from simply hearing. You can't just sit there and let the words flow over you. You have to be continually making sense of the information you're receiving. Thus, even though you're silent and possibly still, you are active mentally. (Just as the much-maligned politicians contend that, even though it looks as if they're asleep in parliament, in fact they're sitting with their eyes closed, concentrating on the debate!) You can't *listen* if you're busy thinking about yesterday's match or tomorrow's disco — though you still might *hear* the lecturer. It could well need a major effort on your part to focus your attention on what is being said — particularly in a traditional lecture given by a poor lecturer. But you must make the effort. Otherwise you might as well be somewhere else, doing something useful or enjoyable, or hopefully both.

You are listening for the main points. But how do you recognise them? Most lecturers use a number of **techniques to highlight the main points**. For example, they may simply repeat an idea, repeat an idea; or say it v-e-r-y s-l-o-w-l-y; or much LOUDER; or with more FORCEFULNESS! Their body language may give some clues: their arms might start waving, or the fist of one hand might start hammering into the palm of the other hand. They may put up an overhead projection slide outlining the main points, or they might take the time to write something similar on the board. The better the lecturer, the more he or she will make use of these audio-visual cues.

However, you can't rely completely on these cues. The only sure way to identify the main points is to **closely follow the arguments** presented in the lecture. Try to distinguish between the following: the main points; illustrations or examples of these main points; other issues that are less central to the overall development of the argument; and irrelevant comments and stories designed to allow members of the audience to rest their brains and their hands for a few moments.

This last comment leads on to the final part of the discussion about what you do in a lecture: listen for the main points and **write them down**. You need a record of the lecture to refresh your memory when you prepare for tutorials, assignments or exams. Without notes you will quickly forget even the main points. This does not mean that you need to write continuously during the lecture. Many major points may already be adequately covered in the textbook or the lecture handouts, and the additional main points may be sprinkled between numerous examples, marginal issues, and irrelevant comments. All you need is the series of major and minor headings used by the lecturer, the major points made under each heading, and one clear example to illustrate each main point. You can, of course, save time by writing in note-form rather than in sentences, and by making extensive use of your own shorthand.

Some students prefer to listen to lectures without the distraction of taking notes. Instead, they list the main points from memory, later in the day. Much depends on the length of time between the lecture and the note-making, and also on what else takes place during this intervening time. Ideally, the notes should be done immediately after the lecture, but this is not always possible. Overall, it makes sense to take *some* notes during the lecture. A bare minimum is the list of major and minor headings which some lecturers display at the start of the lecture.

Another, more popular, school of thought about note-taking is based on the assumption that every point made in the lecture is possibly important, and therefore should be noted down. No lecture is this good! In any case, the tongue is quicker than the hand — at least longhand, and very few students use shorthand. Consequently, you soon find yourself being left behind by the lecturer, and missing major points because you are busy recording minor ones. After an hour of furious writing, you end up with such an unmanageable mass of material that you have to go through your notes and cross out all but the major points.

Occasionally, you may find that although you are noting down only the major points, you are still getting left behind by the lecturer. If this occurs, simply leave space in your notes so that you can add the missing material after the lecture. Sometimes students work in pairs — one taking notes and the other just listening (the jobs can be alternated). If you have this arrangement, then it is usually easy to add the missing points after the lecture.

After the lecture

Some people do no review work of their lecture notes. They assume that the lecture will come flooding back to them after several weeks or months, when they start to prepare for the exams. They are always disappointed! Others adopt a slightly better, but far from ideal, technique and neatly rewrite their lecture notes. On the whole, this is a physical rather than a mental activity: adding missing words to form sentences from notes; underlining headings with a ruler; and so on. But the activity does little to develop an understanding of the material. It is 'busy work' — like colouring in the bars of a bar graph to make it more attractive.

Reviewing your lecture notes requires you to think: to think back to what the lecturer said, and see if you have an accurate record of all the main points; to think about the development of the material, and make sure that you understand the major points, and how they relate to each other; to think about specific questions raised by the lecturer that will be discussed in the next tutorial; to think about issues that initially you found unclear or unsatisfactory; and to think about how the material can be summarised into only one paragraph. You might do this review work on your own, or with one or more friends.

If you prefer to work alone, you may feel that it is a good idea to listen to an **audio recording of the lecture**. Very occasionally lecturers make arrangements to tape their own lectures and have them available for use by students, particularly those who missed the original lecture because of illness. Most of the time, however, you will have to make your own tape recording. Make sure that you have permission from the lecturer before you start taping the lecture. You may be troubled by technical difficulties — lecturers don't always remain behind the lectern, and don't always speak in an easily recorded monotone. Thus, the quality of the recording can be very variable. If you do manage to make a reasonable recording, be very careful about how you use it. Don't go slowly through the tape making a transcript or word for word copy of everything the lecturer said. It will take you far too long and, as with the other take-a-note-of-everything technique discussed earlier, you will produce such a mass of notes that you will have to go through them later and delete all but the major points. Instead, use the recording as an *aide-mémoire* — something to refer to when your memory is hazy about a particular point. Unfortunately, there is the problem of finding on a 1-hour tape a 2-minute segment in which the lecturer covers the point that is causing you difficulties. If you need to find several short segments, you can end up spending a great deal of time over issues that can be cleared up more quickly by talking to fellow students.

I've now suggested on a couple of occasions that you can improve your lecture notes by **co-operating with other stu-**

dents. If you work with another student — one taking notes and the other listening — then getting together to compare notes and thoughts is a normal part of the lecture review process. A simpler technique is to swap notes with someone — though you must be able to read each other's writing! A third technique is to get together with one or more other students, and hold an informal discussion about the main issues raised in the lecture.

Tutorials

At the other end of the spectrum from lectures are those occasions when a student sees a member of staff on a one-to-one basis. The Oxford and Cambridge tutorial traditionally consists of an hourly meeting each week of one or two students and a tutor. The current system in Australian universities and colleges prevents such a generous staff–student ratio! Instead, you are likely to meet your tutor as part of a discussion group of 10 to 20 students (or more). There are two main types of discussion groups: seminars and tutorials. As the distinction between the two is not always clear-cut, I'll first define the terms as I use them in this chapter.

In **seminars** one student takes a leading role by presenting a paper on a chosen topic. In other words, he or she gives a short lecture to the rest of the group. When the presentation is finished, the rest of the group joins in by asking questions and giving comments. I look in detail at seminars in the next main section. In **tutorials** each student is expected to play an equal part. Usually, the main aim is to discuss the topics covered in recent lectures and associated readings. Tutors expect you to come along prepared to talk about the material. The rest of this main section looks firstly at the basic reasons for holding tutorials, and then shows you how to get the most out of your tutorials.

The primary aim of tutorials is to help you **develop a better understanding of the topic under discussion**. You may have problems sorting out a particular point. Hopefully, at least one of your fellow students will be able to explain it. In doing so, this student will improve his or her understanding of the point, as there is no better way to make sure that you really know something than trying to explain it to someone else. The tutorial discussion also helps you integrate what you have heard in the lecture with what you have read in the textbook, and possibly with what appears on TV and in the newspapers.

The second major aim of tutorials is to provide you with an **opportunity to speak in public**. Effective public speaking is a necessary skill for many jobs done by social science and humanities graduates. Indeed, if you consider the job interview as an exercise in public speaking, it is a necessary skill for virtually all jobs. The tutorial is one of the few places where you can practise your verbal skills in at least a semi-formal setting. Answering a straightforward question in a clear and concise way is important. So, too, is the ability to defend your position from criticism in a calm and logical manner.

The third major aim of tutorials is to **encourage contact** between students and their peers, and between students and staff. Tutorials usually widen the circle of people you know, as membership of a particular tutorial group is often the result of chance. For example, some departments simply divide an alphabetical list of students into the scheduled number of tutorial groups. Thus, you are likely to meet people from a wide variety of backgrounds. Tutorials also enable students and staff to get to know each other better. This is important socially, but is also of value academically. For example, a tutor can identify a student who is having academic difficulties, and can thus help to sort them out before they become more significant. A student can give a tutor feedback about the content and presentation of the course, and can thus help staff improve on what they are doing.

Tutors can play a number of roles. At one extreme, some tutors assume leadership of the group. They make it clear that they are in charge, closely direct the discussion, and sometimes give mini-lectures to particularly reticent groups. At the other extreme, some tutors take the role of resource person. They give advice when requested, but otherwise stay silent. Thus, the organisation of the tutorial is left to the student members. Most tutors try to steer a middle course. They prefer to allow people to talk freely, but they will direct the discussion back to the main issues if the group is in danger of being sidetracked. If necessary, they will stimulate a faltering discussion by introducing new issues or presenting controversial viewpoints.

I'll discuss how you can get the most from your tutorials by looking firstly at how to prepare for the tutorial; secondly, at how to participate in the tutorial; and, finally, at how to conduct a review of what you have learned during the tutorial.

Before the tutorial

How do you prepare for a tutorial? Usually, the main aim of the tutorial is to help you develop a better understanding of the topic discussed in a recent lecture. Consequently, it's important to complete all the planning, participation and review activities connected with the lecture.

In addition, you will probably have to do some **reading for the tutorial discussion**. One of the main aims of many lectures is to introduce you to the literature — the books and journal articles that have been written about the subject. The lecturer usually provides you with details of a few of the readings so that you can clarify and extend your understanding of the lecture topic. Sometimes the reading guide refers you to the original account of a social theory or piece of social research. However, its value is limited by the fact that it has been written for other leading theorists and researchers rather than first-year undergraduates. Consequently, the lecturer will often refer you to a textbook which covers the relevant theory or research in a manner more suited to an undergraduate readership.

What is the **best way to use your textbook**? You will usually have two goals in mind: (1) you will want to have a thorough understanding of the material so that you can discuss it at the next tutorial; and (2) you will want to have some adequate notes to jog your memory about the material when you come to prepare for the exam. I'll assume that you have been directed to read specific pages in the text, so that you don't first need to search through the book to identify the relevant sections. You simply have to develop a detailed critical understanding of the main facts and ideas outlined on the specified pages of the textbook.

In many ways, **your task is similar to that facing you in the lecture** — only easier, because you can go through the textbook at your own pace. Recall that in a lecture you first need an idea of its basic structure — the major and minor headings used by the lecturer as a map through new intellectual territory. You

can then either take notes about each of the main points as the lecture proceeds, or you can sit and listen and write your notes from memory after the lecture. Similar approaches can also be used when working with your textbook.

Your first task is to get a general idea of the area covered by the author in the chapter you'll be making notes from. Skim through the pages, looking at the headings of each section. These should also be listed together on the contents page of the book. It's a good idea to write out the headings — to make a contents page for your notes. If you make notes from your textbook as you read through the chapter, one approach is to read a section and high-light the most important points with a pencil. **But how do you identify the important points?** I said earlier that good lecturers emphasise important points by their voice, their gestures, and their use of visual aids. Similarly, good textbook writers make use of different typefaces, marginal notes, and summary diagrams. However, as in a lecture, you can't rely completely on these cues. To repeat earlier advice, the only sure way to identify the main points is to follow closely the thread of the argument. Try to distinguish between the following: the main points; illustrations or examples of these main points; other issues less central to the overall development of the argument; and largely irrelevant comments and stories designed to allow readers to rest their brains for a few moments.

At the end of each section, note down the main points on an A4 sheet of notepaper. Do these notes from memory rather than copying from the textbook. Then check your notes against the highlighted parts of your textbook to make sure that you haven't missed any important points. If you have to add points to your original notes, again do them in your own words. It's an immediate check on whether you really understand the idea, and it's much easier to remember when you prepare for the exams. You then repeat the **sequence of reading, highlighting, note-taking and checking** with each section of the chapter.

Alternatively, you can delay the note-taking stage until you have read through the entire chapter. You should have the series of major and minor headings handy when you come to compiling your notes. Once again, you need to compare your notes with the highlighted parts of the textbook to make sure that you haven't left out anything of importance.

Both techniques are very time-consuming, but you will be working on basic material that needs to be thoroughly understood. You won't regret spending the time: it will help you understand the lectures better; it will help you play a more effective role in the tutorials; and it will save you a lot of time and effort when you come to prepare for the exams.

During the tutorial

What do you do during the tutorial? In the simplest of terms, you can either contribute to the discussion or you can sit there and say nothing. Obviously, there are degrees of participation — from an occasional grunt to a sustained and eloquent defence of a particular point of view. For the moment I will use the basic twofold division of (1) participant and (2) non-participant. Combining these participation categories with two similar categories based on whether or not a student prepares for the tutorial produces the four tutorial roles shown in Figure 1.2: workers, trappists, empty vessels, and drones. I'll discuss each in turn.

Participates in tutorial	Prepares for tutorial	
	YES	NO
YES	Workers	Empty vessels
NO	Trappists	Drones

Figure 1.2   Tutorial roles

Workers

Firstly, there are the students who both **prepare for the tutorial and participate in the tutorial discussion**. Using a beehive analogy, I refer to them as the workers. No tutorial group can function properly without them. These students come to the tutorial having done the class work and private study related to the previous lecture. They have a good understanding of the material; they can, at least, begin to answer any particular questions raised in the lecture or textbook; wherever possible, they are able to relate what they have heard to current events; often they raise questions about what they see as unclear, unsatisfactory, or underdeveloped aspects of what they have heard or read. Moreover, they are willing to share their understandings, insights and questions with others in the group. They know that the only way that the aims of a tutorial will be fulfilled is for members to participate in the group discussion. They appreciate that explaining a point to someone else is the best way to see whether they really understand it; that the best way to see whether their answers to the lecturer's or textbook author's questions are correct is to discuss them with others; and that a useful way to straighten out a particularly puzzling issue is to ask the group about it.

Trappists

Trappists are conscientious students who prepare for the tutorial but, like their monastic namesakes, are **noted for their silence** when the group meets. There are two basic explanations for this lack of participation: some students lack the self-confidence to talk in public, and others have a phobia about public speaking. I'll look separately at each, though many students' lack of participation is probably a reflection of both problems.

Lack of self-confidence Students who lack the self-confidence to talk in public may believe that they are not as intelligent as other students — that anything they say would not be of interest or, even worse, would simply highlight how little they understood compared to the rest of the group. A related problem is the feeling that they don't have the verbal skills to express themselves adequately. They know what they want to say but don't believe they can express it clearly in speech.

Building up self-confidence comes about partly through knowing that you have carefully prepared for the tutorial. It also comes from becoming familiar with the other students in the tutorial. You soon find that you are by no means the only one having trouble with a particular point; or that ideas you thought were too unimportant or obvious to comment on are raised by other group members, and often regarded as valuable contributions; or that other issues you consider important have been missed by everyone else.

There is no doubt that **verbal skills** can vary considerably between students at the start of a tertiary course. Most obviously, there is the gap between those students whose first language is English and those for whom English is a second language. Less obviously, there is the gap between those students whose families and schools have encouraged the development of verbal skills, and those students who have not had the same encouragement. Whatever your background, you will find that your verbal skills develop with *practice*. Take the opportunity to practise in tutorials — that's one of the main reasons why they are held.

Fear of public speaking Although often related to the problem of self-confidence, this phobia does not always have a rational cause. Students with a fear of public speaking may feel confident that what they have to say is of value, but the thought of actually saying it to the rest of the group makes them feel extremely nervous. They get tight-chested and short of breath. This increases their nervousness, as they know they are no longer in a physical state to speak without revealing that they are anxious and tense. To avoid such an embarrassing situation, they simply sit tight. They are in the awkward situation of mentally wanting to participate, but physically not being able to do so. To overcome this phobia of public speaking you need to have control over both your mind and your body.

I'll look firstly at how to **develop the right mental attitude**. Everyone is a little anxious about public speaking. For example, there are countless stories about top performers having stage fright before going on-stage. It is something which improves with experience: the first night is always more nerve-racking than the last. In particular, becoming familiar with the people in the group can help considerably. Over time the tutorial group develops from a formal meeting of strangers to an informal get-together of friends and colleagues. The more familiar and less formal the setting, the easier it is to speak up.

In addition, try to **see the tutorial and your role in it in their true perspective**. There are dozens of tutorials, and scores of comments made in each one. If your nervousness makes you hesitate and stumble, then it's no big deal — you are likely to be the only one who remembers it. The more you exaggerate the importance of any mistakes you might make, the more nervous you become about making them. You can help yourself from starting on this downward spiral by adopting a more realistic idea of the importance of any contribution you might make.

One technique to help you develop a more relaxed mental attitude is called **systematic desensitising**. Fred Orr looks at this in detail in his book *How to Pass Exams* (1984, pp. 38–44). His advice also applies to public speaking situations. You have to write out a series of four or five cards, each outlining in 50 words or so a stage in the process which leads to speaking in a tutorial. For example, the first card might describe the first day of the year: you draw up your timetable on which are your tutorial times and room numbers; and later you go past the room where the tutorials are to be held. The second card describes your preparations for the tutorial, a day or two before it is due to take place. The third describes the period immediately before the tutorial, as you walk into the room and take your seat. The final one describes the tutorial itself, as you sit listening to others speaking and prepare to speak yourself.

You have to relax, then read the first card, imagining the scene in as much detail as possible. You work through the cards until you imagine a scene that causes you to feel anxious. You must then try to wipe the scene from your mind and release the tension by deep breathing and saying *relax* as you breath out. You then again imagine the scene that caused you anxiety. If necessary, you repeat the above process until you can imagine the scene for half a minute or so without feeling anxious. The aim is to work through all the cards without anxiety many times over several weeks.

A second approach to overcoming a fear of public speaking is to try and gain greater **control over your body** to prevent it from becoming so tense. Once again, Fred Orr (1984, pp. 29–38) gives details. In brief, to learn how to relax you must go through a daily program of relaxation training. You find a quiet spot, make yourself comfortable, and gradually relax your body. Your student union or counselling service may well have on loan audio tapes designed to help you relax. Alternatively, you might go along to a relaxation class — there's likely to be some held on-campus or in the local community.

To help you **relax in the tutorial room**, close your eyes, take a deep breath, and let it out slowly while saying *relax* to yourself. Dangle your arms and imagine the tension flowing out through the tips of your fingers. In addition, change your body position once in a while throughout the tutorial, and slowly stretch your arms, back and legs. You *can* do all this without attracting any attention to yourself. Try it and see.

Empty vessels

So far I have discussed workers and trappists. I'll deal quickly with the other two types of student roles listed in Figure 1.2 — the empty vessels and the drones. There is a centuries-old proverb: **empty vessels make the most noise**. Sometimes a tutorial can be afflicted by empty vessels — students who rarely do any of the tutorial preview work but often have a lot to say. Such students have not made the necessary distinction between a tutorial discussion and a chat with friends over a beer in the pub. The important distinction is not where each group meets — indeed, some tutors make a point of avoiding the timetabled room, choosing instead the caf, the pub, or the shade of an old gum tree. The distinction is in terms of the preparation needed for the tutorial. If there are empty vessels in some of your tutorial groups, both the tutors and (more particularly) you and the other students should make them aware of the need for *informed* comment. Otherwise, empty vessels will waste a lot of your time.

Drones

The final group of students, the drones, are named after the male honeybees, which do no work but live in the hive and feed off the honey collected by the workers. As a group, these students are the most difficult to understand. They don't prepare for the tutorial (often boasting about it) and don't participate in the tutorial discussions, but they do turn up for tutorials. Usually their attendance is short-lived as they get bored listening to other students, especially when they can't follow the discussion because they haven't done the necessary preparation. It is up to the participating members of the group to show them the error of their ways. If everyone was like them the tutorial would not get very far.

As a final general comment, it is worth re-emphasising that **the success of tutorials depends on you**. You can't sit back and let others do all the work. Initially, at least, a common failing among first-year students is to assume that it is the tutor's responsibility to ensure that all goes well. Instead, try to see the tutorial as a team effort. The tutor/captain has some organising role, but at the end of the day the result depends on everyone in the team using his or her talents to the full, and co-operating with everyone else. To extend the analogy, the team doesn't cease to function if the captain has to retire hurt. Similarly, the tutorial should be able to continue if the tutor is absent. It won't be quite as easy, but you should still be able to develop your understanding of the topic, to practise your oral skills, and to become more familiar with the other students in the group. If you feel that your group isn't working very well, then the best approach is to try to discuss openly the reasons why. Remember, it's your time that's being wasted if you are part of an unsuccessful tutorial group which staggers along from week to week on the hard work of a minority of its members.

After the tutorial

Finally, I'll look briefly at the tutorial review stage — or what to do after the tutorial. At the very least, spend 10 minutes later in the day thinking back over what occurred in the tutorial. You may have had **your own specific queries** about the lecture or reading. Did the tutorial discussion help you sort out this problem? If so, make a note of what was said. If not, consider whether it's worth following it up privately with your tutor or lecturer. You will get a sympathetic hearing from the staff member, providing that you go along well prepared. (Incidentally, the worst time to approach your lecturer about a point from last week's lecture is just before he or she is about to start on this week's lecture!)

In addition to your own specific queries, ask yourself whether there were any **other noteworthy points** raised in the tutorial. Perhaps someone brought along a newspaper cutting that illustrated perfectly a general point raised by the textbook. Perhaps a new dimension was added to an issue covered by the lecture. Perhaps someone raised an interesting alternative interpretation of some data in the textbook. If so, then make a note of them in your tutorial review session. In particular, take note of the discussion based on any questions specifically prepared by the staff for discussion in the tutorial. Presumably these questions raise important issues, and it's these that also tend to appear on examination papers!

Overall, it's a good idea to **avoid taking notes during the tutorial**. Concentrate instead on listening and talking. If you review the tutorial soon afterwards — and certainly before you go to bed that night — then you should have no difficulty in recalling the important points.

One way of making doubly sure that you recall the important points is to get together with another student in the group and spend a few minutes going over the tutorial. Even better, you might establish a **self-help group** with some of the students in your tutorial. The group need not necessarily confine its activities to tutorial work. You might also want to discuss the lectures, the textbook, and possibly the assignment work. If you do establish such a group, it's best to have a few rules about how it should operate. For example, fix a regular time and meeting place, a maximum period for each session, and possibly a rough agenda of what to discuss.

Seminars

I'll now move on to discuss the third type of class work — seminars. Recall that seminars are usually small discussion groups in which one student takes a leading role by presenting a paper — a mini-lecture — on a chosen topic. When the presentation is over, the rest of the group joins in by asking questions and giving comments. Thus, there are two types of participant in seminars: the presenter and the audience. I'll look at each in turn, again using the same chronological sequence as in the previous two main sections.

Before the seminar

There are two parts to this section. The first looks in detail at the preparation you need to do before presenting a seminar. Usually, you have to give a talk based on an essay which you have to submit for assessment. I look at how to research, plan and write an essay in Chapters 2 and 3. Here, I'll assume that you have completed the essay and concentrate on how you should present it at the seminar. The second part of this section looks briefly at the preparation you need to do before attending a seminar as a member of the audience.

Presenter

Don't assume that because you have written the paper you can simply take it to the seminar and read it out. If you have a lecturer

who reads from a prepared script, you will realise just how ineffective this is. The aim is to **become familiar with your material** so that you can talk about it with only a bare outline of the
main points as a guide. As I show in Chapter 3, you write the
essay using a detailed essay plan which lists the major and minor
headings and the key ideas under each. For example, you may be
asked to prepare a presentation on the following question: 'Why
are there varying rates of illness between social classes?' To present
a paper on this topic, you need to become so familiar with your
material that you can talk for a half-hour or so using only a series
of headings and key points such as that shown in Figure 1.3.
This detailed essay plan is the starting point of your seminar
preparations.

Copy each of the numbered major and minor headings from
the detailed essay plan onto a separate card (150 mm × 100 mm —
or 6" × 4" — cards are best). Altogether you should end up with

---

1. Introduction

2. Describing variations in illness between social classes

3. Explaining variations in illness between social classes
   • Class → Illness, and Illness → Class

   3.1 Radical arguments about the production process
       • dangerous industrial substances
       • general organisation of the production process
       • political environment in which production process
         operates

   3.2 Conservative counter-arguments about the production
       process
       • counter-arguments about dangerous industrial substances
       • counter-arguments about general organisation
       • counter-arguments about political environment

   3.3 Conservative arguments about the consumption process
       • diet
       • smoking
       • preventative health services

   3.4 Radical counter-arguments about the consumption process
       • counter-arguments about diet
       • counter-arguments about smoking
       • counter-arguments about preventative health services

4. Conclusion

Figure 1.3   Social class and illness: detailed essay plan

less than a dozen of these **prompt cards**. Under each heading write down the additional comments listed next to the bullets (•). These refer to the main points that you must cover in your talk. You should also use the prompt cards to remind you about quotations and audio-visual materials. For example, *very occasionally* you might want to quote a particularly important, well-expressed, or illuminating piece from a book or article. If so, you should mark on the prompt card when to read out the quotation, which should be copied out onto a separate quote card and placed immediately after the prompt card.

The use of **audio-visual materials** can improve your presentation. If nothing else, they provide both speaker and listener with a visual focus. Of course, a well-chosen, well-drawn visual image can help convey an idea that might be difficult to describe in words alone. Mark on your prompt cards the times when you intend to show audio-visual aids. Use the blackboard (or whiteboard) to draw only the simplest of diagrams while the seminar is in progress. Prepare all other diagrams beforehand on transparent sheets, and show them to the class using an overhead projector. Your tutor should be able to arrange the necessary materials for you to use.

There are two main ways of producing **overhead transparencies**. The first is to draw them yourself using special coloured pens. Use pens with water-soluble inks in preference to those with permanent colours — if you make mistakes it is much easier to correct them. The main advantage of a hand-drawn transparency is that it shows exactly what you want to show, in colour. The main disadvantages are that it can take a long time to draw, and its effectiveness in part depends on your drawing skills. The second way to produce overhead transparencies is to copy a diagram from a book or article onto a special transparent sheet designed for use in a photocopier. Usually, the original size of the illustration is too small to be copied directly — you need to enlarge the image before taking an overhead copy. The main advantages of the photocopied transparency are the ease with which you can produce it and the quality of the final product. However, you are limited to the illustrations produced by other people, the special photocopy sheets are expensive, and you can produce only black and white images (though you can use coloured pens on the prepared sheets).

Overhead transparencies are particularly useful at the very start and very end of the seminar. When you begin, use a slide to show your major and minor headings — that is, the basic structure of your presentation. When you finish, you are likely to want to raise two or three basic questions arising from the talk which will give the subsequent discussion an initial focus. You can display the questions on the screen for easy reference while the group discusses them. Print the text in large letters or, if you are using a typed copy, make sure that you enlarge it before making an overhead transparency.

When making diagrams for overhead projection slides, aim for maximum size, medium colour, and minimum text. In other words, aim to display an image which is large enough for everyone to see every detail, which uses colour to produce a clearer illustration, and which is uncluttered by unnecessary text. Remember that you *always* add your own verbal commentary — the display is not meant to be looked at in isolation from the talk. Practise how you will take your audience through the display.

More generally, you need to **rehearse your entire presentation**. You must go through your material verbally. Mentally rehearsing your speech is not satisfactory, for two reasons. Firstly, you need to have a clear idea of how long your prepared material will take you. If your presentation is part of a one-hour class, you should talk for no more than 30 to 40 minutes. Less than this and your audience will feel that you have short-changed them; more than this and they are likely to get bored and possibly resentful that you are not allowing them sufficient time to have their say. Because people speak much more slowly than they read, it is important to actually *say* the words to get an accurate estimate of your timing. You may need to add or, more likely, delete sections to fit your presentation into the time-frame.

Remember that a seminar is a semi-formal discussion group and requires the **appropriate level of spoken English**. Rosanna McEvedy and her colleagues in their book, *Speaking in Academic Settings* (1986, p. 29), identify three styles of English: written academic English, spoken academic English, and spoken broad Australian English. Written academic English is very formal, as a reading of any academic journal article shows. Spoken broad Australian English is very informal, as a visit to any pub shows. Obviously, your aim is to use spoken academic English. As a general guide, the level of formality used in this textbook is the level you should aim for when you present a seminar.

You will get some appreciation of what it's like to be a member of the audience if you listen to a tape recording of your speech. If you find your eyelids gently closing as you listen, then you have clear evidence that something is wrong! If you are confident that your material is interesting, then the problem is most likely to be **your voice**. Everyone's voice is unique. As Rudolph F. Verderber points out in his book, *The Challenge of Effective Speaking* (1988), the sound of your voice depends on the pitch (its highness or lowness), volume, speed, and quality (its tone or timbre). You should pay particular attention to how loud and how fast you speak. If you have a very quiet voice, you should practise speaking loudly enough for everyone in the seminar room to hear without difficulty. If you talk very quickly, you should make a conscious effort to slow down your speech. The normal rate is between 140 and 180 words per minute.

A more general problem relates to the way you combine the pitch, volume, speed and quality of your voice. A **monotonous voice** is one in which the pitch, volume and speed remain constant. Because the speaker does not give verbal cues about the relative importance of each word, listeners find it difficult to understand what is said. You can demonstrate the importance of vocal emphasis by choosing a sentence at random and repeating it several times with the emphasis each time on a different word (e.g. *Seminars* are fun; Seminars *are* fun; Seminars are *fun*). At worst, a monotonous voice, like that of the classic hypnotist, can lull the listener to sleep.

A second common problem is to have a **constant vocal pattern** for each sentence, regardless of its meaning. A common British failing is to end each sentence on an inaudible downward pitch. A common Australian failing is to end each sentence with an upward pitch. Usually, a final upward pitch is reserved for a sentence which asks a question. If this vocal pattern is used constantly, it loses this function of identifying a question.

Listen critically, both to others as they speak and to yourself on the tape recording as you rehearse the presentation. Remember, the aim is to match presentation with content: to stress the important words; to distinguish the questions from the statements of fact; and so on. One of the major benefits of basing your presentation on prompt cards rather than reading from a complete script, is that you need to *think* much more about what you are going to say. The more you think, the more expressive your voice will be. The more expressive your voice, the easier it is for your listeners to follow what you're saying.

It is important to be clear about exactly how the seminar will be organised. Firstly, you need to know **who will chair the meeting**. Usually, someone other than the presenter chairs the meeting. The chairperson's role is to call the meeting to order, introduce the speaker, invite discussion questions, and finally thank the speaker. Less formally, the person giving the paper may also have the task of chairing the meeting. The group will probably make a general decision at the start of the course about which format to use. If not, check with the tutor on what he or she has in mind.

Secondly, you need to know **when the audience can ask questions and make comments**. The convention is for the speaker to present the paper, and then for the proceedings to be thrown open for comments and questions. A less formal approach is to allow comments and questions both during and following the presentation. If there is no standard format in your series of seminars, it is up to you to decide how you want to conduct your seminar. On the whole, it is usually easier for the speaker to finish the presentation, and then to respond to questions. You could draw up an initial prompt card, headed 'Preliminaries', to remind you to make clear at the start of your talk the ground rules on which you want to conduct your seminar.

You can also use the preliminaries card to remind yourself to distribute any handouts at the start of the seminar. For example, it is useful to prepare a sheet with the title of the talk and a **100 to 200 word summary**, or abstract. Members of the audience should already have read at least one of the major references, and thus have some background information on the topic of your seminar. The abstract allows them to start matching up their own knowledge with your approach to the topic. The abstract is short enough for most people to read in the minute or two of shuffling and rearranging that always occurs at the start of a class. Your listeners can use the remainder of the sheet to add their own comments during the presentation, and it can be a useful point of reference in the subsequent discussion.

Audience
Finally in this section I'll turn from the presenter of the seminar to

the audience. What preparatory work do you need to do before going along to listen to a seminar presentation? Your preparation is very similar to that for a tutorial. You need to do the recommended reading, noting down the main points and any queries or comments that come to mind. If the seminar relates to an earlier lecture topic, it is also useful to review your relevant lecture notes.

During the seminar

I'll now move onto the presentation of the seminar. This section is a short one, as I've already covered most of the main issues in the previous section. In other words, if you have carefully planned the seminar, you have done most of the hard work before the actual presentation begins. Again, I'll look firstly at the presenter of the seminar and then at the audience.

Presenter

Arrive early at the seminar room to double-check the equipment, clean the boards, distribute the handouts, and, most importantly, compose yourself for the session. Most people feel anxious at this stage, just as an athlete does before the start of a big race. This anxiety is a positive response to your situation — it will help you produce a good performance. If you have been using relaxation and systematic desensitising techniques to overcome your fear of public speaking, you should take a couple of minutes before the start of the seminar to close your eyes, breathe deeply, and relax your body.

Never start by apologising for the quality of your work. If you have prepared thoroughly, apologising is simply not called for; if you haven't prepared thoroughly, it's too late to regret it now.

When **displaying overhead transparencies**, always make sure that the image on the screen is straight and in focus, and that you aren't blocking anyone's view. Don't talk to your audience while you have your back to them — it's bad manners, and much of what you say will be inaudible. Write all important, unfamiliar words on the board. If you're sitting down to present the paper, it's best to draw up a list on the board before you begin; if you're standing, it's probably better to list the words as you refer to them. If there is more than one handout, refer specifically to each one by name or number so that everyone is in no doubt about which handout you're referring to.

Try to **avoid body and speech mannerisms** that might distract the attention of the audience from what you are saying: don't repeatedly scratch the top of your head, fiddle with your pen, adjust your clothes, trace imaginary quotation marks in the air, or pace around the room; and keep expressions such as 'You know' and 'If you like' to an absolute minimum. Try to look around the group as you speak; don't stare at your prompt cards, or at the back wall of the room. If you appear to ignore your audience, they may end up ignoring you.

The first couple of minutes are the hardest. Once you get into your stride it becomes a lot easier. If you've rehearsed your presentation, you should have no **timing problems**. Even so, keep an eye on the wall clock or put your watch on the table in front of you. As you warm to your topic, you may find yourself taking longer than you had anticipated. If so, leave out material rather than speaking more quickly or cutting into the discussion period

AVOIDING BODY LANGUAGE IN SEMINARS

of the seminar. Remember that the discussion period is as much a part of the seminar as the presentation of the paper.

If at the end of your concluding section you **display two or three questions arising from your talk**, these can provide the link between the presentation and the discussion sections of the seminar. Don't try to take the group question by question through the list, like a teacher in a class. The primary purpose of the list is to act as a catalyst for the discussion, not to impose a rigid framework on it. It is likely, at the end of the day, that all the issues will have been discussed, though not in exactly the way you anticipated.

However, occasionally you may feel that the **discussion is getting bogged down**: perhaps it has moved into peripheral or irrelevant areas; or perhaps it is being dominated by one or two talkative individuals. One of the duties of the person chairing the meeting is to ensure that the debate goes smoothly. If you are also performing the role of chairperson (or if you think that the designated chairperson is not doing a good job) then you may have to take a leading role and try to redirect and widen the debate. The displayed list of questions is a useful reminder of how far the debate has strayed from the more central issues raised by your paper.

Of course, **several members of the audience are likely to have comments and questions of their own**. These people are in a similar position to that of someone marking a written essay: complimentary comments rarely take the ideas and arguments presented any further, while critical comments often do. For example, 'I found the talk well-structured and well-presented' can only be responded to by a brief 'Thank you'. Contrast this with the following more critical comment: 'I found what you said to be interesting, but did you really do full justice to the radical interpretations of the issue? If you had, surely your conclusion would have been rather different?' This comment obviously requires a very different response.

The **ability both to give and to take criticism** is an important part of your development as a tertiary student. Don't react irrationally to critical questions — they don't constitute slurs on your personal integrity! In virtually every instance, they will be asked in a co-operative rather than a competitive way, to help develop your material rather than to score points off you. (Points scoring is much more common further up the academic ladder!)

Thus, **consider each question from the audience calmly and rationally.** You are expected to give instant feedback, which can be a problem, especially if you are the sort of person who prefers to look very carefully before you leap. Remember that for the duration of your seminar you are the expert — you have many hours of reading, thinking and writing to draw on. Often, it will be a question of emphasis or interpretation rather than right or wrong. Perhaps you gave the radical interpretations the minor coverage you thought they warranted. Or perhaps you gave them the same coverage as the more conservative arguments, but this point has been ignored or forgotten by the questioner. Or perhaps you deliberately excluded radical arguments from the presentation, for reasons you gave in the introductory part of the talk. Or — just possibly, despite your careful planning — perhaps you should have spent more time on the radical arguments.

You need to weigh up which is the most likely answer and give an appropriate response. Remember that you need to give a reasoned, rational response to all your questioners — even the most mistaken and misguided ones. Thus, if the questioner has simply not been listening properly, or has misrepresented what you said, make sure that you let him or her down gently. Withering scorn is not appropriate! If it is possible that the questioner has a valid point, concede the possibility and try to develop the discussion by asking him or her to expand on the earlier comment, perhaps illustrating the point with a well-chosen example.

At the very end of the seminar, you might want the group to help you **evaluate your seminar**. Sue Habeshaw and her colleagues (1987, p. 39) suggest a very direct evaluation method: simply ask everyone around the table to comment on the content and presentation of the seminar. However, as the book points out, 'the situation is a delicate one', and it's advisable to use the following procedure. Starting with the presenter, each person makes one positive comment and one negative comment about the seminar, without interruption, and without reference to anyone else's contribution. Ideally, the comments should be written down to allow you to consider them at length after the class has finished. Either ask someone to act as secretary for the group, or ask everyone to write down his or her own comments and hand them to you. It may be easier for everyone if the group makes a general decision before the start of the seminar series to conclude each seminar with a round of evaluation comments. If there is no general format, but you would like to hear the comments, then you should mention it at the start of the class. You can remind yourself by adding a note to the preliminaries card.

Audience

What do you do during the seminar when you are a member of the audience? Firstly, make sure that you **arrive on time** for the seminar. If you're late, you either delay the start of the presentation or interrupt the speaker during the important first few minutes. Try to prepare yourself for the presentation by matching up what you have read with the outline provided in the distributed abstract.

Don't look on the half-hour or so of the presentation as time during which you can take it easy. Indeed, when an inexperienced student leads the seminar, you may well be in for a period of hard listening. **Listen actively**. Take notes in the same way you do during a lecture. Ask yourself whether the presentation answers some of the queries you listed before the seminar. Does it raise other issues which you feel need further discussion? If so, bear in mind the ground rules about asking questions: if you have been asked to keep your questions until after the presentation, write them down for future reference.

Be prepared to **play your part in the seminar discussion** — don't sit back and think that you can let the tutor and the presenter do all the work. (If nothing else, it can get very boring watching others talking.) On the other side of the coin, if you are a confident person and the seminar is on a topic that really interests you, be aware of the potential problem of monopolising the discussion period. Convention allows you to ask a question, listen to the reply, and then, if necessary, respond to this reply. If the presenter chooses to comment on your response, you should regard that as the end of the dialogue and allow *other* people either to pursue the issue or to raise other matters that interest them.

Don't avoid making critical comments about the talk, but do it in a manner that's constructive rather than destructive. Generally, comments are best framed as questions, such as the earlier example about '. . . did you do full justice to the radical interpretations of the issue?' Such a format makes it less difficult for the presenter to concede any error or omission, and it also puts you, the questioner, in a less difficult position if it turns out that you have misheard or misinterpreted what the presenter said.

Overall, remember that one day *you* will present a seminar. Participate in other people's seminars in the way that you would like them to participate in yours.

After the seminar

In this short final section, I'll look firstly at what review work you should do after you've presented a paper, and then I'll show how to review a seminar when you have been a member of the audience.

Presenter

You may find that presenting the seminar is an exhausting experience, and thus you may be reluctant to spend time reviewing it later in the day. However, a review period can be very worthwhile in terms of improving both the content of this seminar paper and the presentation of your next one.

The essay on which you based the presentation may have to be handed in for marking. If you have some time between the seminar and the submission deadline, it is useful to recall any verbal or written questions or comments made by members of the audience which will help you to **improve the content of the seminar paper**. Did they highlight any omissions, inconsistencies, confusions, or ambiguities? To continue an earlier example, you might decide to add extra material on the radical interpretations, or perhaps make clearer in the introduction your reasons for leaving them out. If so, you will need to add a note to the end of your reference list acknowledging your indebtedness to the seminar group.

Use your review of this seminar to help you **improve the presentation of your next seminar**. Once again, the final round of positive and negative comments could give you some ideas. In addition, ask yourself the following questions. Did you know your material well enough to feel comfortable presenting the seminar using the prompt cards? Did you make effective use of your visual aids? Did the audience seem to find them helpful? Were you in the best position to use the overhead projector? Did you manage to achieve the right level of formality in your speech? Were you happy with your voice, or did you notice yourself talking too quickly or too quietly, or without much expression? What about your body and speech mannerisms? (Was that student really telling the truth when he said that you used the phrase 'You know' 72 times?) How about the discussion period? Did your questions prove useful? If not, why not? Were you able to keep the audience to the point, and did most people manage to have a say? Did you react coolly to the more critical comments and questions? Was the final round of positive and negative comments a useful evaluation method or a general embarrassment? By asking yourself questions such as these, you can help improve the standard of your next seminar presentation. If you also ask other seminar members, either individually or as part of an informal discussion group, you should get more useful feedback.

Audience

This final comment leads onto what you do as a member of the audience once the seminar is over. In terms of reviewing the content of the presentation and subsequent discussion, your job contains elements of both the lecture and tutorial review work. Thus, you need to think about the **content of the paper** given during the seminar in the same way as you think about any other lecture. Have you an accurate record of the main points? Are you sure about how the main points relate to each other? Are there any points which you still find unclear or unsatisfactory? Does the distributed abstract adequately summarise the talk? What about the discussion of the paper? Were the questions posed by the presenter answered adequately? What about the questions and comments that you jotted down — were the issues dealt with satisfactorily? Similarly, did relevant points raised by other members of the group receive an adequate response?

It is also worthwhile to think about the **presentation of the paper**. Remember that *you* will probably have to lead a seminar during the course of the academic year. Each seminar you attend as a member of the audience will give you some pointers about what to do — and what not to do — in your seminar presentations. Look back over the questions raised earlier in this section: about the presenter's familiarity with the material; about visual aids; about the level of formality and the speed, volume and level of expression in the spoken presentation; about body and speech mannerisms; about the questions used to start off the discussion period; about the reaction of the presenter to critical comments and questions; and about the final round of evaluative comments. Learn from your experience as a member of the seminar audience. Make sure that your next seminar presentation benefits from this experience.

Exams

Your course grade is usually made up of how well you do in your assignments and in an exam. I look in detail at assignment writing in Chapter 3. In this chapter I'll give you some advice about tackling exams. This is appropriate as the preparation, participation, and review stages of your class work are essential to your exam preparation (see Figure 1.1). I'll start with an overview of the topic, looking briefly at the types of exams and the reasons for holding them. Then I'll use the now-familiar before–during–after sequence of headings to structure the advice about how to do well in exams.

Types of exams

The vast majority of Bachelor degree courses include examinations in their assessment program. On average, it is likely that about half your course mark will be based on how well you do in the final examination. The general exam format is such that you have a specified time in which to write answers to a number of questions. Everyone else enrolled in the course is also given the same questions under the same conditions. Under this general definition, there are several types of exam, depending on their basic format and, as a result, on the depth of knowledge they are designed to test (see Figure 1.4).

With **multiple-choice exams** there is a large number of questions, each of which you answer correctly by being able to *recognise* the most appropriate response from a list of half a dozen or so given responses. An example of a multiple-choice question is as follows:

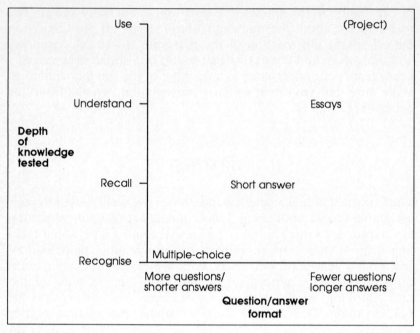

Figure 1.4 Types of exams

Earlier in this chapter, I mentioned the name of an anxiety reduction technique which can be used to help students reduce their fear of public speaking. Is it called:

(a) relaxation therapy;
(b) systematic desensitisation;
(c) stress management reduction (SMR);
(d) public speaking syndrome alleviation;
(e) stage fright phobia alleviation;
(f) adrenalin control therapy?

With **short answer exams** you are expected to *recall* from memory answers to a fairly large number of specific questions. The answers can vary in length. Sometimes you may be asked to supply a single missing word (e.g. 'The technique of gradually reducing your anxiety of activities such as public speaking is termed systematic _____'). Alternatively, you may be asked to write a short answer of one or two paragraphs (e.g. 'Outline the technique of systematic desensitisation').

With **essay exams** there are a number of relatively general questions, of which you usually have to answer no more than half a dozen, writing several hundred words (or more) on each. For example: 'Discuss the technique of systematic desensitisation, paying particular attention to its relative effectiveness compared to other anxiety reducing techniques'. With essay questions you have to show not only that you can recall what you have read or heard, but also that you *understand* it. As Phillip L. Bandt and his colleagues point out, you demonstrate your understanding by 'being able to explain things in your own words and to compare, contrast, and criticize the concepts and ideas with which you are working' (1974, p. 43). Essay exams can vary in terms of whether or not you know the questions beforehand, and whether or not you are allowed to prepare your answers while consulting notes, books and articles (see Figure 1.5).

With **traditional essay exams** you enter the examination room equipped only with pens and pencils, and you find out the exact questions only when you read the examination paper. It's likely that this traditional method is still the one that you will come across most often in your degree course. However, traditional

Can reference materials be used?	Are questions known?	
	NO	YES
NO	Traditional	Open-question
YES	Open-book	(Essay assignments)

Figure 1.5   Types of essay exams

exams are often criticised for their artificiality — it is the only time when you are expected to write without direct access to other sources of information. Consequently, the argument runs, traditional exams place a premium on memorising rather than understanding information.

It is largely in response to this criticism that some staff have introduced **open-book essay exams**. In an open-book exam, you can take reference materials into the examination room, but you still don't know the exact questions until you read the paper. In practice, there is very little difference between traditional and open-book exams. This is because, in the limited exam period, you cannot spend much time consulting your notes and other reference materials. You have to know them thoroughly in order to prepare and produce an essay in less than one hour.

Another alternative is the **open-question essay exam**, where you are shown the exam paper some time before the exam and can thus prepare for specific questions. However, you can't take notes and other reference materials into the exam room. I use open-question exams as I believe they retain most of the benefits of traditional exams, but reduce the main cause of exam stress — the uncertainty about exactly what questions will appear on the paper.

In theory, there is a fourth type of exam — an open-book/open-question exam. In practice, this is identical to an essay assignment where you have a known, specific question and a submission deadline.

(Notice that I have included project work in Figure 1.4. Of course, projects can't be classified as exams, but they do logically follow on in the sequence of multiple-choice, short answer and essay exams. This is because the project report is a long answer to a single question which requires you to *use* your existing knowledge to help you carry out original research, and thus add to the total store of knowledge in the social sciences and humanities. Advanced work of this kind is not expected in the first year of a Bachelor degree program, and thus isn't included in this introductory textbook.)

Why exams?

Why is there such an emphasis on examinations in an undergraduate course? I'll start by assuming the need for *some* type of assessment — that there needs to be a check on each student's level of learning, for use most directly by staff and the students themselves, but also by prospective employers and the public in general. Given this need for assessment, why are exams so popular? (Among staff, that is!)

Firstly, **exams encourage you to read widely** throughout the course. The argument runs that without the stimulus of an exam, you might end up concentrating almost exclusively on your assessed assignment work, and would thus end up knowing a lot about a little. With an exam, you are encouraged to take an interest in a much wider range of issues so that you also end up knowing at least a little about a lot. Of course, it can be argued that at tertiary level such an external stimulus should not be needed — that you should be interested in most of your coursework, and that if you need prodding with the threat of an exam you shouldn't be doing the course.

Secondly, **exams ensure that what has your name on it has actually been done by you**. With assignment work, the name on the face sheet needn't necessarily be that of the person who has done most of the work. In exams, to paraphrase some computer jargon, 'Whom you see is whom you get it from'.

Thirdly, **exams are a convenient form of assessment**. The exam period is a non-teaching period, meaning that marking can be done largely free of the disturbance of formal class teaching and informal student consultation. Moreover, the practice in many institutions is not to return the marked exam scripts to students. Consequently, lecturers can mark papers relatively quickly as they don't have to write comments on the papers as they read them. Exam papers are also convenient to moderate. Moderation is a procedure whereby someone otherwise unconnected with the course checks to see if students have been assessed fairly. This is much easier to do when exams are set: there is only one exam paper to look over; all the students' answer sheets are available for inspection; and, because of the general overlap of answered questions, several sets of answers can readily be compared.

How can you maximise your chances of doing well in an exam? I'll discuss the skills that you need to develop under the now-familiar sequence of before–during–after, or preparation–partici-pation–review.

Before the exam

Your first job when preparing for an exam is to **find out all you can about the exam paper**. The initial course unit handout should give you information about the duration and format of the exam. If not, ask the co-ordinator for details. If the format is to be similar to that of previous years, you will probably find old exam papers available in the library.

It is also helpful to **find out the administrative system re-lated to exams**. For example, what arrangements are possible if you are ill on the day of the exam; or if you are ill for much of the period leading up to the exam but are well on the actual exam day; or if you become ill during the examination? If you find out how the system works, and know in advance what your options are, you are in a much better position to cope effectively with any crisis.

You might also **find out how your result is processed**. In other words, what happens once your paper has been marked and the results of your exam and assignments are added together? There are two main ways in which your result might be pro-cessed. Most simply, the total mark is placed into one of several grading categories. For example, in the department where I work, staff use 50% as a minimum pass mark, 65% as a minimum credit mark, 75% for a distinction, and 85% for a higher distinction. Your grade depends entirely on your *actual* mark, regardless of how well or badly anyone else has done. Thus, once you know your total assignment mark you can easily calculate the minimum exam mark needed for a particular grade.

A second system has a fixed proportion of students falling into each grade (e.g. 10% of students are awarded distinctions, 20% credits, and 50% pass grades, while the remaining 20% are classi-fied as having failed). The basic assumption is that student ability will remain constant from year to year, whereas exam papers vary in their degree of difficulty and staff vary in their marking standards. Under this system, you are competing against other students as it is your *relative* mark, rather than your actual mark, which is of significance. You cannot work out the minimum exam mark needed for a particular grade as you can with the fixed grading category system.

The key to doing well in exams is to **start your preparations early** — the first day of the term or semester is about right! This isn't as crazy as it first sounds when you bear in mind that class preparation, the classes themselves, and the class reviews are all part of exam preparation (see Figure 1.1). In other words, the reading, thinking, writing, listening and speaking necessary for you to get the most out of your classes make up most of the work that you need to do for the exams.

In an earlier section I noted that many students have a fear of public speaking. Similarly, many students have a **fear of examinations**. Sometimes the fear is well-founded — they haven't done the necessary preparation and their exam answers will highlight this. Often, however, the fear is more irrational in that students are well prepared, at least in terms of their knowledge of the course content. If you are one of this group of students, you should spend time using the relaxation and systematic desensitisation techniques mentioned in the section on tutorials.

Of course, you will need to refresh your memory by going through your notes in the couple of weeks before the exam. What you do in this revision period will depend largely on what sort of exam you have to do. Recall that **multiple-choice exams test recognition, and short answer exams test recall**. Consequently, to prepare for multiple-choice and short answer exams you need to become familiar with the fine detail of your notes. For example, a short answer exam set on this chapter might include the following questions:

(a) What is the recommended number of hours for a full-time study week?
(b) What does Elizabeth Hastings (1984, p. 8) mean by 'contaminated time'?
(c) List three techniques designed to ensure that lecturers talk for no more than 15 to 20 minutes without a break.

(d) List the pros and cons of taping a lecture.
(e) What is the recommended procedure for taking notes from a textbook?
(f) Describe the four main student roles in a tutorial.

In contrast, **essay exams test your understanding** of your material. Consequently, in order to prepare for essay exams you need to become familiar with the big picture rather than the fine detail. For example, an essay exam set on this chapter might include the following questions:

(a) Use the preparation–participation–review model to illustrate the range of study skills required by tertiary students to get the most from their lectures, tutorials and seminars.
(b) In order to be a successful student you have to be well organised. Discuss.

Overall, with multiple-choice and short answer exams, you need to memorise a large number of facts and figures but you are not

expected to make many connections between them. With essay questions, you need to know fewer facts and figures but you are expected to connect the main points to make a single, coherent statement.

For all exams, of course, you need to memorise information. It is immediately evident in multiple-choice and short answer exams when you don't know the facts and figures, and it doesn't take much longer in essay exams for a marker to realise that even the most elegantly constructed essay has been built on a very thin foundation of knowledge. As Fred Orr (1984, pp. 74–76) points out, improving your memory is basically a question of using **the 4Rs — reading, reciting, (w)riting and repetition**. Firstly, you read your notes. Do it actively. Have a pencil in your hand and a jotting pad next to you. Write down important words and phrases (making sure you spell them correctly) and make lists of the main points or headings. This will help reinforce what you have read and discourage your mind from wandering. Next, you need to look up from your notes and try to remember the main points. Reciting, or saying the words out loud, helps you fix them in your mind. Check back to your notes if you get stuck, and do a final check of the entire section. Next, write down your own version of the section from memory. There is no need to spend time writing the points out in full — brief notes will do, providing you know what goes under each heading. (Be honest with yourself!) When you have completed the entire reading–reciting–(w)riting process, repeat the sequence as many times as you can, bearing in mind the limited time available, the other notes that need memorising, and just how difficult you find the material to learn. A revision timetable is useful.

John Wade (1990, Chapter 11) suggests that you can memorise material that you already understand by using **the concert technique**. The basic idea is that by listening simultaneously to both speech and music, you use both halves, or hemispheres, of your brain to help you memorise the material. You need two cassette players (or one with a dubbing facility). Use one to record yourself reading your study notes. Break up long sentences into shorter sections, pausing after each section. Make each pause equal in length to the previous spoken phrase by repeating the phrase silently to yourself while leaving the tape running. Use the second tape to play gentle instrumental music as you're listening to your study notes. Close your eyes and relax whilst listening, and let any images form in your mind while the concert is in progress. John Wade suggests that you spend about 10% of your study time using the concert technique.

Preparing for multiple-choice and short answer exams

For these exams you will spend virtually all your exam preparation time using the **4Rs and concert techniques**. Use your knowledge about past exams to read your notes with an eye specifically on those details which could be included in these types of exams — lists of technical terms, important figures, definitions, and issues that you can summarise in a paragraph or two.

Occasionally you may find it helpful to use mnemonics, or **memorising devices** (see Higbee 1988). There are two basic ideas behind many mnemonics. Firstly, the more meaningful something is to us, the more likely we are to remember it. Secondly, we memorise information visually and verbally (i.e. in pictures and words). If we can attach a picture to a word we tend to remember it more easily. For example, to remember the six countries of the Association of South East Asian Nations (ASEAN) — the Philippines, Singapore, Brunei, Indonesia, Thailand and Malaysia — you could use the sentence 'Philip sings brilliantly in the mall'. All or part of each word should remind you of the name of a country. You could reinforce your memory with a picture of Prince Philip or Phil Collins (or any other Philip or Phil whose face is familiar to you) giving a thundering performance in your local shopping mall. John Wade (1990, Chapter 10) takes the idea a stage further, suggesting that your imagery should use as many senses as possible. Thus, you might add to the visual image the sound of the singing and the feeling of being part of the crowd. Generally, try to imagine the scene as *vividly* as possible. Make it a video clip rather than a still photograph, and make the scene novel (e.g. Phil Collins singing in the local mall) or even bizarre (e.g. Prince Philip up a pine tree singing in the local mall) rather than mundane.

Describing the process of devising mnemonics makes it appear much more laborious than it really is. Even so, you can spend a considerable amount of time making up suitable mnemonics — time that might be used more efficiently by directly memorising the material. **Limit your use of mnemonics** to those occasions when your usual approach doesn't seem to be working, yet the material is important enough for you to spend more time trying to memorise it.

A more generally useful memorising technique requires the use of a pack of small filing cards. On the front of each card write a term that you want to learn about, and on the back add the definition or the major points that you want to remember. After a while you will have a few dozen of these cards. You can carry them around with you and use them to test yourself any time you have a couple of minutes to spare.

Preparing for traditional essay exams

Essay exams require you to *use* material rather than just recognise or recall it. Consequently, you need to go beyond simply memorising your notes when preparing for these exams. Firstly, **get to know the format of the exam** — its duration, how many questions there are on the paper, and how many you have to answer. You then know how long you can spend on each answer and you can decide on how many topics to prepare. To make sure that you can always produce the required number of answers, prepare twice that number of topics. For example, if you have to answer four questions on the paper, aim to prepare eight topics in your revision.

For each topic covered in the unit, **draw up a list of possible questions** from past examination papers and your lecture, tutorial and seminar materials. Familiarise yourself with the material for the first topic you have chosen to revise using the 4Rs and concert techniques — though there is no need to memorise information at the same level of detail as for a multiple-choice or short answer exam. Then select a question on that topic at random from your list of past and possible exam questions, and from memory try to structure what you know to answer the question. I look in detail at producing an essay plan in Chapter 3. Exam question preparation is similar.

For each question you must first **be clear about what you have to do**. Look at the question, word by word, and make sure that you know what each word means. Also, look at how the words are arranged. Are you asked simply to describe something, or are you also asked to explain it? If it is a complex phenomenon that you are asked to describe, are you given any information about how you should go about it, or do you have to supply your own categories in order to break down the large, complex whole into smaller, more manageable pieces? Similarly, if there is more than one explanation about why something occurs, are any schools of thought mentioned in the question or do you have to supply them yourself?

Devising the basic structure, perhaps as a table or diagram, is the final part of this crucial first stage. From this you have to draw up a **detailed outline plan**, with major and minor headings, and paragraph themes (see Figure 1.3). Where possible, add particularly interesting examples to illustrate a general point. Finally, compare your plan with your notes and see if there are any important points that you have missed. If so, add them to your plan.

When you are satisfied with the structure of your answer, look at each section in turn. **How confident are you about writing out the section in full?** Perhaps you're unsure about the details of a particularly useful illustration or, more importantly, perhaps you really aren't all that clear on a basic argument that you need to outline. Whatever the reason for your lack of confidence, the best way to overcome it is to attempt to write out the section in full, from memory. Compare what you have written with your notes and work on the specific bits where your answer is unclear, misleading, or simply incorrect.

Make sure that you do this type of **active exam preparation**, rather than passively reading the same materials over and over again. You will find that with active revision you end up memorising just as much information and, more importantly, you will have used your notes in a similar way to that required of you in the exam.

One problem with answers in note-form is that it can be difficult to **estimate how much you can cover in the time available** for each question during the exam. The only foolproof way to find out how much you can write in the time allotted is to actually do one or two essays under exam conditions. In other words, you need to write out in full one or two essays without access to reference materials, using a strict time limit. Patrick Dunleavy (1986, p. 151) refers to these as 'timed essays'. Try one of the questions for which you have already prepared a satisfactory answer in note-form. Compare what you covered in the timed essay with the earlier answer in note-form. Obviously, if you are able to cover the material in 20 minutes, you have seriously underestimated the time available. However, you are much more likely to find that the timed essay covers only part of the material in the note-form essay because you have seriously overestimated what you can write in 45 minutes or so. You then have to prune your outline plan to fit the time available. Thus, timed essays can be very time-consuming, but they can prove invaluable if they highlight a major timing problem.

Timed essays also help you to **test how your handwriting stands up to sustained pressure**. Most probably you type or word process your assignments. If so, the exam is the one important occasion in each unit when your handwriting is read by other people. Most of the time your handwritten materials — your class and textbook notes and probably the first drafts of assignments — are for your eyes only. Speed, not clarity, is the watchword — you can decipher your own scribbling even though most other people cannot.

Of course, the exam situation is different. **Speed is still a watchword; but so is legibility**. If your writing is largely unreadable it is largely unmarkable. Staff faced with scores, if not hundreds, of exam papers to mark cannot afford the time to decipher poor handwriting. Check the legibility of your handwriting by asking a friend or relative to read a page of your timed essay — the last page is usually the least legible as you struggle to say all you want to say in the remaining time. If the reader hesitates and stumbles over words, then the message to you is clear — fewer words, greater legibility.

You can also look at the **clarity with which you have expressed your ideas**. Once again, asking the opinion of someone else is very useful. Try to arrange a swap system with another student in the same course. Such an arrangement benefits both of you and means that the essays are read by someone with the necessary background in the discipline. If you are working on your own, look critically at each paragraph. Where does each lie on a 7-point scale from crystal clear to utterly garbled? Can you express what you want to say in a more direct, simpler style? Is a paragraph vague basically because you don't really understand what you are writing about? Do certain words or phrases keep appearing which don't really have any real function — the literary equivalent of 'You know' and 'I mean' in speech? Examiners aren't looking for finely-honed pieces of literature, but they do expect (and reward) clarity and directness.

Preparing for non-traditional essay exams

Preparation is similar for **open-book essay exams** as for traditional closed-book exams. As I pointed out earlier, because you have so little time in the exam, you must be virtually as well prepared for an open-book as for a traditional exam. The only difference might be in the number of facts and figures you memorise to illustrate your general ideas. Providing that you have ready access to such information in your notes, you can minimise the amount of such detail you need to memorise.

Preparation for **open-question essay exams** is more focused because you already know what the essay questions will be. To encourage wider reading, staff who use this type of exam sometimes hand out a longer list of questions from which they select the ones for the exam paper. For example, I have a list of eight questions from which I select six, and expect students to answer four. If any of your course lecturers use this method, it is important that you work out the optimum number of questions to prepare. In the above example, if you prepare six questions then, regardless of which questions are on the exam paper, you will always be able to answer four of them. If you prepare only five questions, it's possible that you will be able to answer only three of them, one less than you need. If you prepare seven questions you will always be able to answer at least five questions, one more than you need. Because you know the specific questions, you can prepare specific answers. Of course, outline plans are still important, as are timed essays. As your task is more focused when preparing for open-question exams, the examiner will expect a higher standard of answer in terms of both content and presentation.

During the exam

I'll now move on to give some general advice about what to do during the exam. The first step is to **get to the right place at the right time, and in the right frame of mind**. Give yourself plenty of time to travel to the examination room. If you arrive early, use this time to exercise your body (and, hopefully, relax your mind) by taking a brisk walk around the block. Alternatively, you might find a quiet seat in the library and spend some time practising a relaxation technique. Either activity is certainly better than hanging around outside the exam room with a gaggle of hyped up students, all busy increasing their level of nervous tension!

When you take your seat in the exam room, **check the physical conditions** of the place where you will spend the next three hours or so. Is your table unsteady? Is the sun streaming in on you? Is it too dark to read or write satisfactorily? Is there a radio playing in an adjoining room? Is the clock not visible from your seat? If problems like these occur, try to get them fixed before the exam begins — don't just grumble to yourself. If you can, solve the problem yourself. If not, explain the problem to the supervisor and ask that something be done to correct it. Remember, the next few hours are important ones.

You might be allowed to read through the paper some time before you can start writing. **Make maximum use of reading time.** Before looking at the questions, read very carefully through the instructions at the top of the paper about what you must do. How much time do you have? How many questions must you answer? If the paper is divided into sections, how many questions need answering from each section? Are any questions compulsory? Do you have to start each question or section in a separate booklet? You should already know most of the answers to these questions but it's important to double-check. What you do next obviously depends on whether you're faced with an essay exam or a short answer exam.

Essay exams

If it's an essay exam, read quickly through the paper and **make a mental note of the probable, possible, improbable and impossible questions**. Then read each question in more detail, starting with the probables and working through to the impossibles, and check to see whether your initial evaluation of each question was the correct one. You should be able to convert at least a couple of the probables to definites so that you can start planning your first answer immediately the written part of the exam starts. Detailed planning of a question is best left until you have a pen in your hand, but you can do some brainstorming work when you evaluate each question during the reading time. You could well come up with some particularly interesting and novel ideas during this session. Jot them down as soon as possible

— good ideas, particularly under exam conditions, tend to surface and then sink without trace if you don't grab hold of them.

Never start writing your answer without an outline plan. Think of the essay as an intellectual journey. Hopefully, you are familiar with most of the route you will take, having already been along parts of it during your exam preparation. Even so, it's a fairly complicated journey and, unless you're very lucky (or doing an open-question exam), you won't have taken this exact route before. In such circumstances it's useful to have a map to consult as you go along. The outline plan is your map. If there is no jotting pad available in the exam room, pull out the middle two sheets of the answer booklet and use these to draw up each of your outline plans. As you write your answer and turn over to a new page, you can carry the outline plan with you and glance across to it as you write. If you write the plan in the answer booklet you have to keep flicking back to it to check on what comes next. This can interrupt your train of thought.

Keep an eye on the time. It is likely that you will spend a bit longer on your first answer than on your last, but don't end up with only 10 minutes to do the last question when you really need 30 minutes. A law of diminishing returns applies to exams — if a question is marked out of 20, it is relatively easy to get the first five marks, a bit harder to get the next five, considerably harder to get the next 5, and next to impossible to get the final five. Don't waste valuable time trying to squeeze out the final few marks for one question when you could be better employed on another question, earning the first 50% of the marks. For example, you may have to complete four questions in three hours, an average of 45 minutes per question. Spend no more than 50 minutes on each of the first three questions, thus allowing you a minimum of 30 minutes to complete the last question. If you find that you have still not finished a question after 50 minutes, then finish the paragraph you're working on and leave a space in the answer booklet so that, time permitting, you can return to it later. If you do eventually have some time after you have completed the final question, go back and try to finish any question that you abandoned earlier. Obviously, the more practice you have with timed answers, the less likely you will be to run over time.

Use all the available time. If you complete the final question and there are still several minutes remaining before the end of the exam, read quickly through what you have written, looking for glaring errors caused by the speed at which you wrote the material. Any additional time can be spent on looking at answers in more detail, correcting errors, omissions, duplications and illegible words.

Multiple-choice and short answer exams

These exams are more straightforward, though the earlier comments about timing and checking still apply. Diana Percy gives some hints for doing multiple-choice tests in her book *Study Tactics* (1983). They include the following. Firstly, make sure that you read *all* the options before selecting the most appropriate answer. Remember that some answers may be more appropriate than others. Secondly, bear in mind that the *more* restrictive the statement, the *less* likely it is to be correct. For example, be wary of options which include words such as 'always' and 'never'. Conversely, the less restrictive the statement, the more likely it is to be correct. Finally, beware of extra-long or jargon-riddled options. In other words, don't work on the principle that the less you understand a possible answer, the more likely it is to be correct! Of course, the best way to make sure you choose the right option is to know the right answer.

After the exam

I'll now look very briefly at what to do when an exam is over. You may well have several more exams to prepare for, perhaps another on the following day. Even so, you have just finished what was probably a gruelling three hours, during which time you were working under exceptionally high pressure. **Give yourself a chance to unwind.** Take at least an hour to do something completely different, whether it's running on the beach or watching a video.

Before moving on to the next round of exam preparation, find 10 minutes or so to **look back over your performance** in the last exam to see if it gives you any ideas for the next one. For example, if you had virtually no time to do the final question, don't use this review period to mentally kick yourself about the marks lost. Instead, use the experience to reinforce the need for timing your answers. Perhaps the basic problem was that you hadn't written any timed essays when you were preparing for the exam. Use your experience from the last exam to give you a clearer idea of just how much material you can cover in the next exam. Make a note that next term or semester your exam preparation will definitely include timed essays!

Further reading

There are many books about study skills. Some useful Australian texts include:

Dixon, J. 1988, *How to be a Successful Student Without Quitting the Human Race*, Penguin, Ringwood.

Hastings, E. 1984, *How To Study at Tertiary Level,* Thomas Nelson, Melbourne.

Marshall, L.A. & Rowland, F. 1981, *A Guide to Learning Independently*, Longman Cheshire, Melbourne.

Orr, F. 1984, *How To Pass Exams*, Allen & Unwin, North Sydney.

Orr, F. 1988, *How To Succeed at Part-time Study*, Allen & Unwin, North Sydney.

For a rather unconventional approach to study skills, look at the following book which, you may recall, I referred to earlier when discussing memorising techniques:

Wade, J. 1990, *Superstudy: A New Age Guide*, Dellasta, Melbourne.

John Wade's general approach is reflected in the following examples: using a plumb-bob (a weight on a string) to show what your 'deep mind' thinks (p. 35); enhancing your ability to learn through massage and acupressure (p. 42); and improving your learning by 'embodiment' (p. 83) — moving your body in a way that reminds you of the topic you're working on.

2

Library skills

Introduction

As a tertiary student, you are part of a worldwide academic community. Like you, everyone is busy writing. Of course, the vast majority of this writing, like your essays, is read by only a handful of people, but even the tiny proportion that is published represents an enormous volume of material. For example, in Britain alone, each year it takes 13 kilometres of shelving to store a single copy of every new book. Overall, as Adams and Schvaneveldt (1985, p. 51) point out, it would take several years to read what's produced in a single day.

Even when you take out all those publications that are of no interest to social science and humanities students, all that are now outdated, and all that are not written in English, you are still left with an **enormous amount of literature**. Somewhere in this literature are books and articles which will provide useful facts and ideas for your next essay. The only problem is finding some of them! Fortunately, your college or university library provides you with a first-rate navigational system — providing you know how to use it. This chapter is designed to be a library user's manual. Of course, like all manuals, it will begin to make complete sense only with hands-on experience.

To use a library effectively and efficiently you need to **become familiar with the library's resources, and how they are organised**. For example, you need answers to a host of basic questions relating to the rules of the library. How do I become a registered library user? When is the library open? Can I borrow books any time that the library is open? How many books can be borrowed at one time? What is the loan period? Can I renew books by telephone? Is there an after-hours book return system? How do I reserve a book? How do I operate the photocopiers? Can I bring a bag or briefcase into the library and, if not, are there lockers where I can safely store my belongings?

All libraries have staff specifically employed to assist readers. Make sure that you know where to find these librarians and, if you get stuck, ask for their help. Particularly at the start of a new academic year, the number of readers requiring assistance can be large and you should be prepared to queue for service. Many queries are answered by the various information pamphlets available in most libraries. Check these before you stand in line.

Finally, you need to become familiar with the geography of the library — in particular, to know how the library's collection of materials is organised. Obviously, each library is unique, but I can make some general points about the two main items in every library — the book and journal collections.

Books

The librarian's basic job is to make the library's collection of materials as accessible as possible for prospective readers. In part, this is achieved by shelving each book according to its subject. A major task of a cataloguer is to classify books by subject area. Cataloguers use several classification schemes, though two predominate: the Dewey Decimal System, and the Library of Congress System.

The **Dewey Decimal System** is the one most commonly used in Australian academic libraries. It is based on 10 broad classes, each class having 10 divisions and each division having 10 sections (see Figure 2.1). Most books of interest to social scientists are in the 10 divisions of the 300 class. For example, if you are doing an economics degree course most of your interest will be focused on the 330 division, the 10 sections of which represent more specialised areas of economics (e.g. 331 is 'Labour economics'). Although not shown in Figure 2.1, each section can, in turn, be broken into even more specialised areas by adding more numbers after the decimal point (e.g. 331.1 is 'Labour force and market', 331.11 is 'Labour force', and 331.118 is 'Labour productivity').

Classes	Divisions of social sciences	Sections of economics
000 Generalities	→ 300 Social sciences	→ 330 Economics
100 Philosophy etc.	310 General statistics	331 Labour economics
200 Religion	320 Political science	332 Financial economics
300 Social sciences ⎯	330 Economics ⎯	333 Land economics
400 Language	340 Law	334 Cooperatives
500 Natural sciences etc.	350 Public administration	335 Socialism etc.
600 Technology	360 Social problems etc.	336 Public finance
700 Arts	370 Education	337 International finance
800 Literature	380 Commerce etc.	338 Production
900 Geography & History	390 Customs etc.	339 Macroeconomics etc.

Source: Dewey Decimal Classification, 1989.

Figure 2.1   The Dewey Decimal System, using the example of economics

If you are a psychology or geography student, you will have noticed that your subject is not referred to in the 10 social science divisions shown in Figure 2.1. With the major exception of social psychology (302), psychology books are classified in the 150s (e.g. 156 is Comparative psychology). Non-regional human geography texts are scattered throughout the social sciences class, and regional geographies are classified in the 910s, according to region (e.g. 915 is Asia).

The **Library of Congress System** is much less widely used in Australian academic libraries. It uses letters to identify 21 main classes (e.g. D is 'History: General and Old World', H is 'Social Sciences' and J is 'Political Science'). A second letter is used to denote subdivisions within each class (e.g. HT represents 'Communities, Classes, Races', and JC represents 'Political Theory'). Further subdivisions are made by adding numbers to the initial letters (e.g. HT51–500 deals with communities, and JC571–628 deals with the state and the individual).

In addition to categorising books by subject, librarians often use three other criteria to divide the book collection. Firstly, most libraries have a **reference collection** in addition to the main collection. The reference collection includes encyclopedias, dictionaries, university and college handbooks, atlases, and some of the various publications mentioned later in the chapter (e.g. *Australian Public Affairs Information Service,* and *Social Sciences Citation Index*). All these items are for dipping into rather than for reading from cover to cover, and thus are not available for loan. Secondly, many libraries have a separate **collection of the most popular books**. Often access to this collection is tightly controlled — the place where the collection is housed may be off limits to borrowers with library staff operating a counter service to supply requested books, and the time the books are available on loan may also be strictly regulated with relatively heavy fines for late returns. Thirdly, **oversized books and small pamphlets** (i.e. items which are much larger or smaller than usual) are often shelved together at the beginning or end of a section, rather than being integrated with the other books in the section.

Finally, I'll define some terms relating to books that you may well come across — edited books, editions and monographs. An **edited book** usually includes several chapters on related themes, each written by a different author. Each author is invited to contribute a paper using certain guidelines specified by the editor concerning the exact topic, the length of the chapter, and various points about writing style. In addition, the editor may contribute an introductory chapter and, possibly, a concluding chapter.

An author may revise and update an existing book which continues to be sold under the original title. However, it is designated as a **new edition** to show that it's substantially different from the earlier version. If a reading list specifies a particular edition of a book, make sure that it is this edition that you use — the edition number is usually shown quite prominently on the front cover, and the year of publication also distinguishes it from earlier editions. (I'll say more about this in the next chapter.) If you use a different edition, any page numbers referred to in the reading list are likely to be incorrect. If you do find the relevant page numbers, you cannot be certain that the author has maintained his or her views about this particular topic.

A **monograph** is a book with a single theme. A book analysing a very specific topic written by a single author is the archetypal monograph. However, with a suitably wide interpretation of the idea of a single theme, all non-reference books can be defined as monographs. In other words, most of the time 'book' and 'monograph' are interchangeable terms.

Journals

While at high school you may have used information from recent newspapers and magazines to make your essays more topical.

You should also apply what you read in the daily newspapers and weekly news magazines to your university or college work. In addition, you are expected to use the specialist academic magazines. These publications are usually referred to as journals, periodicals or serials. Like their more popular counterparts, they all have the basic purpose of keeping their readers up-to-date with what is going on. There are hundreds of journals potentially of interest to social science and humanities students. For example, in Australia alone there are over 200 journals in the social sciences and humanities. Some of these are listed in Figure 2.2.

Journals are usually issued several times each year. Publishers use a variety of **ways to identify each issue**. Most common is the volume and number system. All issues published within a specified time period, usually one year, are part of the same volume. Within a volume each issue is given a different number. Thus, the combination of volume and number gives a unique reference number for each issue of the journal. In addition, all journals show the year of publication and many of them also show the month of publication.

Abacus
Accounting and Finance
Architecture Australia
Australian Archaeology
Australian Economic Papers
Australian Economic Review
Australian Feminist Studies
Australian Geographer
Australian Geographical Studies
Australian Historical Studies
Australian Journal of Communication
Australian Journal of Education
Australian Journal of Linguistics
Australian Journal of Philosophy
Australian Journal of Politics & History
Australian Journal of Psychology
Australian Journal of Public Administration
Australian Journal of Social Issues
Australian Law Journal
Australian Literary Studies
Australian & New Zealand Journal of Criminology
Australian & New Zealand Journal of Sociology
Australian Psychologist
Australian Quarterly
Australian Social Work
Australian Society
Community Health Studies
Current Affairs Bulletin
Journal of Australian Political Economy
Journal of Australian Studies
Labour History
Meanjin
Media Information Australia
Melbourne Journal of Politics
Melbourne Studies in Education
Politics
Quadrant
Regional Journal of Social Issues
Social Alternatives
Social Analysis
Urban Policy & Research
World Review

Figure 2.2 Some Australian social science and humanities journals

Each issue includes several **articles**. Articles may present the results of some original research based on surveys, field work or laboratory work, or they may provide a critical review of other people's research and theories. Articles can vary in length but most journals specify a maximum of around 5000 words. Articles are usually preceded by an abstract — the main points summarised in a few hundred words. Occasionally, an article will produce a response from someone who disagrees with what the original author has said, and the original author, in turn, may then write a rejoinder to the critic's response. Most journals also include a **book review section**; indeed, some journals contain little else but book reviews. A review is designed to give some idea of the content of a book, to praise its good points, criticise its bad points, and generally say what, if anything, the book adds to the existing literature on the same topic.

A library often has a **specialised area to display current issues of journals**. (The same also applies to new books.) The journals are ordered either alphabetically or by using the library's standard classification scheme. It is useful to put aside at least an hour or so every month to browse through this display. You may find something that is particularly useful for your current essay, but the main purpose is simply to try and develop a basic idea about what is occupying the minds of some of the top people in your chosen area. Look especially at the abstracts — they are there to give the busy reader, such as yourself, a good idea of the basic message of the article. Occasionally, you will come across something that looks interesting enough for you to spend time reading the article in full. Even more occasionally, you might find a review that prompts you to track down and read the original book.

When a new issue is published the previous issue is stored with the rest of the **back copies** making up the library's holdings of this journal. In some libraries, all journals are shelved together in a special collection; in others, the journals are shelved alongside the books. To reduce the chances of loose issues of a journal being lost or stolen and to increase their durability, individual issues making up a complete volume are often bound in a distinctive hard cover. Usually these are not for loan.

Sometimes, back copies of journals are stored on **microfilm** as they are cheaper to buy than paper copies and take up less shelf space. Space is particularly important with daily newspapers (imagine the size of a pile of newspapers containing a few years' back copies of the *Age* or *Sydney Morning Herald*). The drawback is that to read the microfilm you need to use a microfilm reader. These machines can be fiddly to set up and expensive to use if you want to do some photocopying. However, librarians are aware of the problems and will help you set up the machine and photo-copy material as effectively as possible. It takes only a few tries before most people become proficient at using microfilm readers.

Having made some general comments about books and journals, I'll now consider how, from the hundreds of thousands of books and articles in your university or college library, you can find the dozen or so items that will be of most use to you when preparing your next essay. At the broadest level, most library searches fit into one of four categories, depending on whether or not you're looking for books or journal articles, and whether or not you're using a lecturer's reading list showing information such as author, title and year of publication. However, because it's useful to deal with government reports separately from other books, Figure 2.3 shows six basic types of library search: looking for books with and without a reading list; looking for journal articles with and without a reading list; and looking for government reports with and without a reading list. The rest of this chapter follows this outline, giving some examples of the main library tools — catalogues, encyclopedias, bibliographies etc. — that can help you with your search. Figure 2.4 shows some of these.

Type of material	Using a reading list	
	Yes	No
Book	✔	✔
Journal article	✔	✔
Government report	✔	✔

Figure 2.3   Basic types of library search

Locating books

During most of your book-hunting expeditions to the library you will have a valuable piece of equipment — the reading list provided by each of your course lecturers. Usually, finding books from these lists is relatively straightforward once you have become familiar with your library system. In addition, there will be occasions when you need to go further than the items on a

---

A. With a reading list

Books, articles and reports

1. Your library's author/title catalogue (books and reports)
2. Your library's serials list (journal articles)
3. Other nearby tertiary libraries
4. Other nearby libraries (public, TAFE, academic staff)
5. Inter-library loan system

B. Without a reading list

Books

1. Your library's subject catalogue
2. Special encyclopedias and dictionaries, e.g.
   International Encyclopedia of the Social Sciences
   Social Science Encyclopedia
   Penguin Dictionary of . . .
3. Bibliographies, e.g.
   Australian National Bibliography
   Subject Guide to Books in Print
   British National Bibliography

Journal articles

1. Indexing journals, e.g.
   APAIS
   Social Sciences Index
   British Humanities Index
   Social Sciences Citation Index
2. Abstracting journals, e.g.
   Applied Social Sciences Index and Abstracts
   Sociological Abstracts
   Psychological Abstracts

Australian government reports

   Australian Government Publications
   ABS *Catalogue of Publications and Products*

Figure 2.4 Finding books, journal articles and government reports

prepared reading list. For example, you may be writing an essay and find that you have little or no information about one of the topic areas on your outline plan. In this situation you need to find out which books and articles may be useful, and whether your library can supply them. I'll look at how to handle each of these situations.

Locating books from a reading list

At the end of each chapter in this text there is a short list of books for further reading. For example, at the end of this chapter I refer to *The Student Sociologist's Handbook* by Pauline Bart and Linda Frankel. I'll go through the process of how you might try to find this book. Firstly, you need to find out whether or not your library has a copy. If it does you need its call number (i.e. its Dewey or Library of Congress classification number). Once you have the call number you can work out which shelf it is on. If your library doesn't have a copy of the book you might try getting a copy elsewhere. I'll now look at this procedure in more detail.

Most academic libraries now use **computer-based catalogues**, which are generally referred to as On-line Public Access Catalogues or OPACs. Computer-based catalogues are menu-driven — that is, they present you with a menu, or list of options, and you have to indicate your choice. Make sure that you follow *exactly* the instructions shown on the screen. The main menu gives the basic options and it is from this that you start a catalogue search. All main menus give you the option to search by title and author, and the display will probably show you exactly how to type in the information (e.g. 'Bart, P' not 'P. Bart'). However, if you have both the title of the book and its author, it's usually more straightforward to enter the title, especially if there are likely to be several authors in the catalogue with the same surname and first initial (no problems with a name like Burdess, of course!). If the book title starts with 'A', 'An', or 'The', leave out this first word when keying in the title. If you don't, you may be told that the book is not in the collection, even though you saw it on the shelf last week.

If the machine lists the book you're looking for, follow the instructions on the screen to obtain the **call number**. If your library uses the Dewey system, the call number of the Bart and Frankel book is likely to be 301.07, the classification number for this type of general social sciences text, followed by either BAR or B283s for Bart, the principal author (i.e. the first author listed on the cover of the book). If your library uses the Library of Congress classification system, the call number is likely to be HM68 (i.e. a general sociology text) followed by B37 (for Bart). Note down the entire number — it saves time in the long run. If your library operates a popular loan scheme the catalogue should tell you whether this book is in the popular collection or in the main collection. A computer catalogue may also tell you if the book is already out on loan and, if so, when it is due back.

You need to use the call number to **find the book on the shelves**. First locate the relevant general area of shelving and then follow the number order (301.05, 301.06, 301.07, or HM66, HM67, HM68) until you find the specific subject area. All the books in this area (i.e. all with a 301.07 or HM68 call number) are shelved alphabetically by principal author. Most of the time you will find your book on the shelf without any problems.

But what **if the book is missing**? There are several possible courses of action. One is to throw up your hands in despair, convince yourself that you didn't really want the book anyway, and make a hurried exit from the library to more inviting parts of the campus where what you want *is* available — like a cup of coffee. This option is not recommended! A more useful strategy is to scan the shelves around the spot where the missing book should be. Books are sometimes rather carelessly reshelved by previous readers in *about* the right spot but not *exactly* the right spot. Of course, you are someone else's 'previous reader'. Make sure that you either reshelve books accurately or put them in the appropriate place for reshelving by library staff.

If the book is not on the nearby shelves there are a number of courses of action. If the catalogue does not give the loan status of each book, check at the issue desk to see if it is on loan. If it is, you might want to reserve it when it is returned. Another possibility is that it is in the popular collection and either you missed the notice in the catalogue or, possibly, the catalogue has not been updated. Check to see if it is there. Other possibilities are that it is being used by someone else in the library, or that it is waiting to be reshelved. If you don't track it down in the meantime, you should recheck the shelf in 24 hours. If it is still not there, it is possible that the book has been stolen or totally misshelved, either accidentally or by some idiot wanting to make sure that no-one else finds it.

If the book has gone missing, or it has never been purchased by the library, you might want to widen your search to include **other tertiary libraries**. Many academic libraries are now part of a larger network. For example, the CAVAL (Co-operative Action by Victorian Academic Libraries) Reciprocal Borrowing Scheme aims 'to enable staff and students of participating libraries to borrow from libraries other than their own, thereby improving their access to library materials' (CAVAL 1990, p. 4). Virtually all Victorian academic libraries are members of CAVAL. Find out whether your library is part of a wider network. If it is, arrange for a borrowing card and information booklet. Make sure that you check opening times and borrowing restrictions in the information booklet before going to another library. It could save you considerable disappointment and frustration. Some academic libraries share the same computer catalogue. If your library is part of such a scheme, you can find out which of the other participating libraries have a copy of the book you're looking for, and get its call number from the catalogue before going to borrow the book.

If you can't travel to another tertiary library, check out **other local libraries** — the public library, the TAFE college library and the library of the lecturer co-ordinating the unit. The chances of finding the book at the public library or TAFE college are not high — but you never know. If you do find the book in the TAFE library, it's likely that you won't be a registered TAFE borrower and thus won't be able to take the book home. However, you should still be able to read the book in the library and photocopy the important sections. Another possibility is that your lecturer will have the book. Many academics have relatively large personal libraries, though not all are keen to lend books to students, claiming that their libraries would be smaller and grubbier if they did! However, not all take this view and you may well get a sympathetic response, especially if you can show that the book is important and that you have tried elsewhere.

A final option is to borrow the book through the **inter-library loan scheme**. The problem here is that it can be both costly and slow. You may be required to pay at least part of the handling and postage costs, and you may not get to read the book for perhaps a fortnight. Obviously, an inter-library loan is an option to take when all else fails.

Of course, you could use a bit of lateral thinking and move away from searching for a particular book towards looking for a book on a particular subject. As librarians classify books by subject, **all books on the same topic are shelved together**. Consequently, if you move your attention away from the gap on the shelf (representing the missing book) and towards the books on either side of the gap, the chances are you will come across a book that is just as useful as the missing one.

Locating books without a reading list

As I pointed out earlier, when you are trying to find a book using someone else's reading list, you simply need to find out if your library has the book and, if so, where it is located. Without a reading list your search starts further back, as you must first draw up your own reading list. In other words, you need to search through the published books to find those on your particular subject. There are three possible ways of conducting this search: (1) using your library's subject catalogue; (2) using specialised encyclopedias and dictionaries; and (3) using publications which list books according to subject. I'll consider each in turn.

Your library's subject catalogue

The best way of searching for books on a particular subject is to use your library's subject catalogue. This is different from the author and title catalogues mentioned earlier. The subject catalogue lists various subject headings in alphabetical order, and under each heading are included all the relevant books in the library's collection. For example, Figure 2.5 shows the subject headings related to the general topic of sex discrimination which are listed in the subject catalogue of my library.

Under each subject heading are details of all relevant books held in the library. Like the subject headings the books are listed alphabetically by the surname of the principal author. Figure 2.6 shows details of one of the books listed under the heading of 'Sex discrimination in employment — Australia'.

You need to **write down part of the catalogue entry** to enable you to find the book on the shelves. It is a good idea to use 127 mm × 76 mm (or 5" × 3") indexing cards like those traditionally used in a library's card catalogue. Note down those details which you will need later should you use the book in an essay and need to include it in a reference list. You need the authors, date of publication, book title, publisher and place of publication. (I'll say more about these in the next chapter.) It's useful to write down information from the catalogue in the format shown in Figure 2.7. The author's name goes at the top of the card to make it easy to

```
Sex discrimination
Sex discrimination against women
Sex discrimination against women — congresses
Sex discrimination against women — developing countries — congresses
Sex discrimination against women — history
Sex discrimination against women — law & legislation — Australia
Sex discrimination against women — United States
Sex discrimination against women — United States — history
Sex discrimination in education
Sex discrimination in education — Australia
Sex discrimination in education — congresses
Sex discrimination in education — Great Britain
Sex discrimination in education — United States
Sex discrimination in education — Victoria — Melbourne
Sex discrimination in employment
Sex discrimination in employment — Australia
Sex discrimination in employment — congresses
Sex discrimination in employment — United States
Sex discrimination in insurance — Australia
Sex discrimination — juvenile literature
Sex discrimination — law & legislation — Australia
Sex discrimination — Victoria — periodicals
```

Figure 2.5   Headings from a library subject catalogue

```
Game, Ann.
Gender at work/Ann Game & Rosemary Pringle, photography
by Helen Grace. — Sydney : George Allen & Unwin, 1983. —147p.,
(12) p. of plates : facsims; 23 cm. — (BRN: 77074)
        WI 331.41330994 G192g C.1
        WI 331.41330994 G192g C.2
```

Figure 2.6   Subject catalogue entry under 'Sex discrimination in
employment — Australia'

```
GAME, A. & PRINGLE, R. 1983

Gender at Work,
George Allen & Unwin, Sydney

331.41330994 G192g
```

Figure 2.7   Layout of your catalogue cards

sort the cards into alphabetical order by the principal author, and
the layout of the other information makes it easy when you come
to type out the reference list. The Dewey (or Library of Congress)
number is needed to locate the book on the shelves.

Of course, only a limited number of subject headings are used by cataloguers. For example, 'Library orientation' is a subject heading but 'Library user orientation' is not. Therefore, you must know the correct headings before you can make maximum use of the subject catalogue. This is especially important with a computer-based catalogue where, unlike a card catalogue, you can't always scan the subject entries on either side of the first one you try. Most libraries use the list of headings devised by the Library of Congress in Washington, DC. It is a long list of over 160 000 headings, taking up three hefty volumes entitled (not surprisingly) ***Library of Congress Subject Headings (LCSH)***. These volumes, or their microfiche equivalent, are usually found in the catalogue area of the library. Figure 2.8 shows an extract from *LCSH*.

Figure 2.8 shows in bold type the heading 'Socialization'. Any books in your library's collection dealing with 'the process by which individuals are taught to function in the group and share group values and patterns of behavior' (the *LCSH* definition) will be included in the subject catalogue under the heading 'Socialization'. In addition, the *LCSH* entry gives guidance about broader terms (BT) and narrower terms (NT). For example, you may find some

---

Socialization
Here are entered works dealing with the process by which individuals are taught to function in the group and share group values and patterns of behavior.
UF　　Child socialization
　　　　Children — Socialization
　　　　Enculturation
　BT　　Acculturation
　　　　Child rearing
　　　　Education
　　　　Ethnology
　　　　Sociology
　NT　　Assimilation (Sociology)
　　　　Cognition and culture
　　　　Manchester scales of social adaptation
　　　　Political socialization
　　　　Social learning
　　　　Social skills
　　　　Women — Socialization

Source: Library of Congress Subject Headings 1988, p. 3490.

Figure 2.8　Extract from *Library of Congress Subject Headings*

books about socialisation listed under the broader term 'Accul-turation'. Similarly, if you look under the narrower term 'Assimila-tion (Sociology)' in the subject catalogue you may also find mate-rial concerned with socialisation. The UF symbol means 'Used For'. It shows that the heading in bold type has been used for, or instead of, those listed alongside the UF symbol. For example, there is no authorised heading 'Child socialization', any books on this topic being listed under the more general heading of 'Socialization'. Anyone turning to the entry 'Child socialization' in the *LCSH* is directed to 'USE Socialization'.

Specialised encyclopedias and dictionaries

Another way of searching for books on a particular subject is to use a number of specialised encyclopedias and dictionaries, which you'll usually find in the reference collection of your library. Most provide a summary (sometimes several pages long) and a short bibliography, or list of books, on the topic. The eighteen-volume ***International Encyclopedia of the Social Sciences*** (*IESS*) is the major social science encyclopedia. As with all reference books, the more general the topic, the more likely you are to find it listed. For example, *IESS* has entries dealing with education, envi-ronment and political participation, but not the Victorian educa-tion system, the Australian Conservation Foundation or the Queensland electoral system. Another point to note is that such a mammoth publication is not updated very often — the *IESS* was published in 1968.

More compact, and more recent, is the single-volume ***Social Science Encyclopedia*** which was published in 1985. With over 900 pages this encyclopedia provides a very useful introduction to over 700 different topics. For example, if you wanted some basic ideas on Fascism, the *Social Science Encyclopedia* gives a 1000 word summary and lists three books for further reading. It also directs you to two other related entries in the encyclopedia. If you wanted an introduction to mental disorders, there is a 2000 word account followed by 10 books for further reading and reference to four related entries.

Even more compact, but more specialised, are the various **sub-ject dictionaries** such as the Penguin series, which includes eco-nomics, geography, political science, psychology, and sociology. For example, in *The Penguin Dictionary of Sociology* (Abercrombie,

Hill & Turner 1984) there are about 500 entries ranging from 15 to 1500 words. There is a cross-referencing system with a list of other relevant headings at the end of each entry. In addition, many entries have suggestions for further reading from an extensive bibliography. For example, there is a 300 word commentary under the heading 'Nuclear Family', followed by a list of related terms (e.g. 'Conjugal Role', 'Patriarchy') and three books recommended for further reading. You should consider buying your own copy of a subject dictionary, particularly if your course concentrates on one discipline area.

Bibliographies

The third option for searching for books on a particular subject is to use specially prepared lists of books, or bibliographies. The basic list used to locate Australian books is the ***Australian National Bibliography*** *(ANB)* which lists recently published Australian books and pamphlets. There is a subject index in which books and pamphlets are arranged under Library of Congress headings. For example, you can use *ANB* to find Australian books dealing with the issue of abortion. The subject entries from the most recent edition at the time of my library search are shown in Figure 2.9A. Although there are two entries, both refer to the same report which is concerned with both 'Abortion counseling' and 'Abortion services'. (Note the American spelling of counselling in the *ANB* heading to match the US-based Library of Congress subject headings.) The Dewey number (363.46099423) refers you to the main part of the bibliography where books are listed by their Dewey classification number. The entry in this classified sequence is shown in Figure 2.9B. It includes all the information you need to obtain a copy of the report.

Often, the classified sequence can be used to extend the search to books on related issues. Recall that earlier I suggested that because all books on the same topic are shelved together in the library, you can often benefit from looking at the books on either side of the particular one you set out to find. Similarly, in the *ANB* classified list of books you can often usefully scan the entries on each side of the one found using the subject index.

If you want to find books that have been published outside Australia, the single most useful bibliography is ***Books in Print*** which lists most non-fiction books published in the USA (and

---

A. Extract from the Subject Index

Abortion counseling — South Australia
Working Party to Examine the Adequacy of
Existing Services for the Termination of
Pregnancy in South Australia. Report of
the Working Party to Examine the Adequacy
of Existing Services for the Termination
of Pregnancy in South Australia
363.46099423
Abortion services — South Australia
Working Party to Examine the Adequacy of . . .

B. Extract from the Classified Sequence

363.4'6'099423
**Working Party to Examine the Adequacy of
Existing Services for the Termination of
Pregnancy in South Australia.**
Report of the Working Party to Examine
the Adequacy of Existing Services for the
Termination of Pregnancy in South
Australia. — (Adelaide) : South Australian
Health Commission, 1986. — vi, 116, (24)
p.,(1) p. of plates : col. map ; 30 cm.
Spiral binding.
Bibliography: p. 109–116.
ISBN 0 7243 4319 9 : price unknown
1. Abortion services—South Australia
2. Abortion counselling—South Australia
I. South Australian Health Commission. II. Title

Source: ANB 1989, pp. 4 and 281.

Figure 2.9 Extracts from the *Australian National Bibliography*

books imported to the USA which have a sole US distributor). As you might expect, *Books in Print* is a much larger publication than the *ANB*. This is partly because of the much larger publishing industry in the USA, and partly because it includes all books that are still in print, regardless of their original publication date. *Books in Print* is published in three parts listing books by author, title and subject. It is the *Subject Guide to Books in Print* which you will need to track down American books on your essay topic.

The ***Subject Guide to Books in Print*** comes in four hefty volumes, totalling nearly 8000 pages and listing over two-thirds of a million books under nearly 66 000 subject headings. However, despite its size it is very straightforward to use. Library of Con-

gress subject headings are listed alphabetically, and under each subject heading books are listed alphabetically by author. The sheer number of books is astounding. For example, in the 1989–90 edition, there are 18 valid subject headings relating to abortion with a total of 335 separate entries. Even under the very specific heading of 'Abortion—Religious Aspects—Catholic Church' there are 15 books and pamphlets listed.

As you might expect, the direct British equivalent of the *Australian National Bibliography* is the **British National Bibliography** *(BNB)*. The latest edition I looked at was on microfiche, a medium increasingly used by publishers of large-scale and continually changing bibliographies. *BNB*, like its Australian counterpart, requires you to find a Dewey number in the subject index and to use this to find the main entry in the classified sequence. For example, if you want to locate books about how Catholics view abortion, you will find in the subject index the heading 'Abortion—Catholic Viewpoints'. This refers you to section 261.83 in the classified section. In the 1988 edition of *BNB* there are two entries under this number — a 32-page pamphlet and the proceedings of a conference held in Scotland in 1987.

As the last example indicates, it is often much easier to track down details of potentially useful books and pamphlets in bibliographies than it is to get hold of the books themselves — particularly if they have been published overseas. The best strategy is to **use your own library's subject catalogue first** — at least you know that books listed there are fairly readily available. If you draw a blank with the subject catalogue, move on to the *Australian National Bibliography* on the assumption that Australian publications are most likely to be held by Australian libraries. If you continue to be unsuccessful, you might then look at the *Subject Guide to Books in Print* or the *British National Bibliography*. However, bear in mind that if you do find a book listed which seems relevant, you will have to use another library to obtain a copy. If you don't have the time or money to go along to another library or to use the inter-library loan system, then it is pointless spending time using these bibliographies.

Locating journal articles

Once again, your lecturer may have done the hard work and given you a list of journal articles — you simply have to find where they are stored in the library. Alternatively, you may have to draw up your own list of journal articles and then find them in the library. (Not to mention having to read and understand them, make notes from them, and use them in your essays!)

Locating journal articles from a reading list

Equipped with sufficient information about a journal article — author, title and journal details — you should be able to track it down very quickly once you have **become familiar with your library's system of shelving journals**. Most libraries have an alphabetical list of their journal titles which also tells you the call number of each. It is also likely to give details of when the library started buying each journal and whether any volumes are missing. It's worth checking these details as they could save you a wasted journey (e.g. it's pointless going to the shelves to look for the 1980 edition of *Australian Quarterly* if your library's collection doesn't start until 1982). If your library doesn't have a copy of the journal article you're looking for then you need to cast your net wider to include nearby tertiary libraries, other local libraries and, if necessary, the inter-library loan system.

Journals may be shelved either in a special serials collection or distributed throughout the main collection. **If the journals have been bound**, the covers will show the year and volume, and it is easy to pick out the one you're after. However, be aware that several numbers, or issues, are bound together and that some journals start each issue at page one. Thus, it may take a little while for you to find the article as you first have to find the appropriate issue (using the issue number or month) and then find the right pages within that issue.

Unbound copies of journals, particularly ones which are published weekly or monthly, can quickly become disorganised as readers mix them up as they reshelve them. Don't expect that the November 1990 issue will always be sandwiched between the October and December 1990 issues. You may have a fairly long search through dozens of issues before you find the right one. On the other side of the coin, do your bit to minimise the general level of frustration in the library by making sure that any unbound journals that are in order stay that way!

Locating journal articles without a reading list

How can you discover what articles have been published on a particular subject? One possibility is to amble through the serials collection until you come across a likely-looking journal title, and then to flick through some recent editions hoping that something will turn up. This is not recommended! Nor is the slightly less inefficient procedure of looking down the library's alphabetical list of journals, identifying a likely title and flicking through some recent editions.

Collections of journal articles can be very large. There are about 200 Australian journals covering the social sciences and humanities. If each journal publishes about 25 papers annually, then each year sees an extra 5000 Australian articles of potential interest to you. Looking back over the last 10 years, there is thus a pool of around 50 000 potentially useful articles published in Australia alone. Add on all those from other English-speaking areas and you quickly begin to calculate in the hundreds of thousands. Without help you have little chance of finding those journal articles which are of particular interest.

Enter the librarian! To improve your access to this mass of information, librarians have produced a number of **reference journals listing articles by subject**. There are two types of reference journal: (1) indexing journals which list the author, title and journal details; and (2) abstracting journals which, in addition to the above, also provide an abstract of each article. Indexing journals tend to be relatively broad in scope. Abstracting journals are more specialised, most concentrating on a particular discipline. I'll provide examples of both types, but they will start to make real sense only when you begin to use them yourself.

Indexing journals

You will probably make most use of an indexing journal with the rather off-putting title of *APAIS: Australian Public Affairs Information Service: A Subject Index to Current Literature. APAIS* is compiled by staff at the National Library of Australia, who describe it in the introduction to each edition as 'a subject guide to scholarly periodical literature in the social sciences and humanities published in Australia, and to selected periodical articles, conference papers, and book and newspaper articles on Australian economic, social, cultural and political affairs'. Eleven fairly slim monthly issues are replaced with an annual cumulative volume. *APAIS* uses subject headings listed alphabetically. Under each heading there are articles listed alphabetically by title.

An example will help demonstrate that *APAIS* **is easy to use**. Imagine that you want to find out what articles have been published recently in Australia about how university and college students cope with stress. I suggest that you work backwards from the most recent edition of *APAIS*. Usually it is necessary to look at several of the monthly editions for the current year before you work back to the most recent annual edition. When I made this search, there were 10 monthly editions (from October 1989 back to January 1989) and the most recent annual edition was for 1988.

There is an *APAIS Thesaurus* — an alphabetical list of subject headings — but usually there is sufficient guidance in the *APAIS* volumes themselves. For example, when I looked under the heading 'Students' in the October 1989 edition of *APAIS*, I was directed to a number of narrower terms, one of which was 'Students, Terti-ary'. (Similarly, if I had looked under the heading 'Tertiary Students' I would have been directed to 'Use: Students, Tertiary'.) There were six articles under this heading. The only one relevant to the search for papers on how students cope with stress is shown in Figure 2.10.

The *APAIS* entry shows that an article entitled 'Undergraduate student stress and coping strategies' (which includes a bibliography and tables) was written by James C. Sarros and Iain L. Densten, and was published in the journal *Higher Education Research and Development*, volume 8, number 1, in 1989 on pages 47–57. In brackets at the end of the entry are the subject headings assigned to the article. Starred subject headings show that the article is listed in *APAIS* under that heading. Thus, the Sarros and Densten article is concerned with 'Students, Tertiary', 'Stress (Psychological)' and 'Surveys', and is listed twice in *APAIS* — under 'Students, Tertiary' and under 'Stress (Psychological)'. You may wish to widen your search and look also at articles under 'Stress (Psychological)', though most will be concerned with groups other than tertiary students (e.g. the October 1989 list included articles about members of the armed forces, railway workers, and lecturers). A second way to widen the search is to use the related terms listed at the end of each group of articles under a subject heading. For example, the two terms related to 'Students, Tertiary' are 'Education, Tertiary' and 'Graduates'.

Don't get the idea from this example that you can always find relevant articles so quickly! Indeed, if you have a fairly specific topic you may have to look in several editions, both monthly and annual, before you find something of interest. For example, I had to go back to the 1987 annual edition of *APAIS* before I came across

---

Students, Tertiary
Undergraduate student stress and coping strategies. bibl., tables. SARROS, James C. and DENSTEN, Iain L. Higher Education Research and Development, v. 8, no. 1 1989:47–57 (Students, Tertiary)*/Stress (Psychological)*/Surveys

---

Source: APAIS October 1989, p. 92.

Figure 2.10   Extract from *APAIS*

another article specifically on stress among tertiary students (Fogarty 1987).

In the USA, the direct equivalent of *APAIS* is the *Public Affairs Information Service*. However, because of the much larger volume of material published in the USA, a more useful tool is the more specialised **Social Sciences Index** *(SSI)*. According to its standard prefatory note, *SSI* covers over 350 journals 'in the fields of anthropology, economics, environmental sciences, geography, law and criminology, planning and public administration, political science, social aspects of medicine, sociology and related subjects'. Quarterly issues are replaced by a cumulative annual volume.

The format is similar to that in *APAIS* with subjects listed alphabetically, and articles under each heading also listed alphabetically by title. Again, as with *APAIS*, you are directed away from headings which are not used towards headings which are. You are able to widen the scope of your search by using the listed related headings. For example, under the heading 'Social research' you are advised to '*See* Social science research; Sociological research'. Then under the heading 'Social science research' you are advised to '*See also*' a range of related topics including 'Anthropological research', 'Economics research' and 'Political science research'.

In the UK the main indexing journal for the social sciences and humanities is the **British Humanities Index** *(BHI)*. It indexes articles from over 300 British newspapers and journals. Quarterly issues are replaced by an annual volume. Again, subjects are listed alphabetically and the articles under each heading are arranged alphabetically by title. Guidance is also given on valid and related terms. For example, under the heading 'Pop Music' you are advised to 'see Music, Popular', and under the heading 'Gambling' are listed the related headings of 'Coin-in-the-slot Machines', 'Horseracing' and 'Lotteries'.

Finally in this discussion of indexing journals I'll look at the **Social Sciences Citation Index** *(SSCI)*. It is published three times each year, the last one being an annual cumulation. It is slightly more complicated to use than the other indexing journals. This is partly because it is more comprehensive, completely indexing 1400 journals and selectively indexing 3300 journals. A second reason is that *SSCI* is four indexes in one: the Permuterm Subject Index lists authors by the subject of their articles; the Source Index lists authors alphabetically; the Corporate Index lists authors by geographical location and institution; and the Citation Index lists where an author has been cited by other writers. Don't be put off by the rather daunting appearance of *SSCI*. With a bit of practice it is quite easy to use, especially when, as I show below, you use only the subject and author indexes.

A search for journal articles on a particular subject begins with the **Permuterm Subject Index**, so-called because it lists all possible *permu*tations of the pairs of key *terms* in the title of an article. For example, the article 'Drinking-related beliefs of male college-students' (Johnson 1988) is listed under four main headings — 'Drinking-related', 'Beliefs', 'Male' and 'College-students'. Under each heading the same article is referred to three times, the other three headings appearing as subheadings (e.g. 'Drinking-related' is paired with 'Beliefs', 'Male' and 'College-students'; and 'Beliefs' is paired with 'Drinking-related', 'Male' and 'College-students').

Of course, with the previous example I have put the cart before the horse — I went from the article to the subject index. The Permuterm Subject Index is designed to help you go from a subject heading to a journal article on that subject. For example, you might be preparing an essay on the social consequences of divorce. One of the main sections in your essay plan is about the effect of divorce on the children of divorcing couples. However, you find that this topic is not adequately covered by the books and articles on the lecturer's reading list, and so you need to find some extra material. The annual Permuterm Subject Index of *SSCI* for 1988 has 'Divorce' as a main heading, followed by dozens of associated words listed alphabetically, from 'Abortion' to 'Year'. One of these associated words is 'Children', under which are listed the names you see in Figure 2.11.

Each person listed (Bornstei. MT, Connell HM etc.) is the principal author of an article which includes the keywords 'Divorce' and 'Children' in its title. You have to follow up the details of the articles in the **Source Index** which lists authors alphabetically. I'll follow up the first name on the list — Bornstei. MT. Notice the full stop between the surname and the initials. This shows that the name has been shortened because it is longer than the eight character spaces reserved for each author's surname. This is of no practical importance when it comes to following up the author in the Source Index — the first eight letters of the surname, plus the initials, plus the two keywords in the title of the article, allow the correct entry to be pinpointed easily in the Source Index. Figure 2.12 shows the entry you're looking for.

```
DIVORCE
CHILDREN  — — —→    BORNSTEI. MT
          — — —     CONNELL HM
          — — —→    DEMAESEN. B+
          — — —→    DEUTSCH CP+
          — — —→    GLENN ND
          — — —→    JOHNSON CL
          — — —→    KALTER N+
          — — —→    PAQUIN G
          — — —     SANDER E
          — — —→    STREET E+
          — — —→    WEITZMAN M
```

Source: SSCI Annual Permuterm Subject Index 1988, column 3177. Reprinted with permission of the Institute for Scientific Information® (ISI®). Copyright 1989®.

Figure 2.11 Extract from the Permuterm Subject Index of *SSCI*

```
BORNSTEIN MT
BORNSTEI. PH WALTERS HA — CHILDREN OF DIVORCE —
EMPIRICAL-EVALUATION OF A GROUP-TREATMENT PROGRAM
J CLIN CHIL 17(3): 248–254 88 42R P9824
          UNIV MONTANA, MISSOULA, MT 59812, USA
```

Source: SSCI Annual Source Index 1988, column 1172. Reprinted with permission of the Institute for Scientific Information® (ISI®). Copyright 1989®.

Figure 2.12 Extract from the Source Index of *SSCI*

The Source Index entry shows that the paper was written by M.T. Bornstein, P.H. Bornstein (I assume the shortened surname is also Bornstein) and H.A. Walters. The title of the article is 'Children of divorce — empirical-evaluation of a group-treatment program'. It is in the *Journal of Clinical Child Psychology* — 'J Clin Chil' is explained in a list of abbreviations at the front of the Source Index. The article is in volume 17, number 3, on pages 248–254, and was published in 1988. There are 42 references (42R) to other articles and books in the paper. The final number on the line (P9824) is a catalogue number should you want to buy a copy of the article from the publishers of *SSCI*. On the next line is the professional address of M.T. Bornstein. It is an accepted academic practice to write and request a copy of an article. Authors often obtain from the publisher of the journal several dozen copies (or reprints) of their papers, specifically to send to people who request a copy. However, it may take several weeks for the reprint to arrive, so it

is rarely useful if you want the reprint to help you with an essay that is due in 10 days time!

Recall that Bornstein is only the first of eleven authors listed in the Permuterm Subject Index under the keywords 'Divorce' and 'Children' (see Figure 2.11). You would be likely to follow up several more of these entries in your search for suitable material. Some articles could well alert you to interesting new ideas. For example, the article by Glenn is entitled 'The marriages and divorces of the children of divorce'. You may not have thought of this longer-term issue when drawing up your essay plan on the social consequences of divorce. Seeing the entry could well prompt you to add a new section and attempt to track down Glenn's paper (or at least an abstract of it).

Note the cross and arrowhead symbols in the Permuterm listing of authors (see Figure 2.11). A cross (+) after the name indicates a review article. For example, the three papers by Deutsch, Kalter and Street are all reviews of a book by W.I. Hodges entitled *Interventions for Children of Divorce: Custody, Access and Psychotherapy*. The arrowhead (→) indicates that this is the first time that the following author's name appears under the main heading (in this example, 'Divorce'). So, for example, if you look further down the list of words associated with divorce, and find 'Bornstei. MT' without the arrowhead, you will know that it is another reference to the paper in the *Journal of Clinical Child Psychology* which you have already tracked down.

It is important to **look under other subheadings**. As the Permuterm Subject Index is computer-generated, you will find very similar terms listed separately — the computer identifies them as different words and therefore puts them in different sections. For example, under the main heading 'Divorce' you will find not only the subheading 'Children', but also subheadings for 'Child', 'Childrens' and 'Childs' (not to mention 'Daughters', 'Families' and 'Family'). Similarly, in addition to 'Divorce', other main headings include 'Divorced', 'Divorcees' and 'Divorces', all with at least the sub-heading 'Children'. To tap the full potential of the *SSCI* you have to spend some time sorting through these cross-references. However, it will be time well spent as you are likely to come across at least one reference to an article which is both highly relevant and available in your library.

Abstracting journals

Having gone through the main indexing journals, I'll now look briefly at abstracting journals. These are similar to indexing journals in that they provide bibliographic details of journal articles listed by subject. They are different from indexing journals in that they also provide an abstract, or summary, of the main points of the article. The abstract gives you a good guide as to how useful the article will be to you: whether it is likely to be of major use to you and worth reading in full; whether it is of minor use to you and only worth noting what is said in the abstract; or whether it is of no use to you at all.

ASSIA: Applied Social Sciences Index and Abstracts is one of the few general abstracting journals serving the social sciences. *ASSIA* started in 1987. It is published every two months with an annual cumulative volume. Each year *ASSIA* lists over 20 000 articles from 550 English language journals from nearly 20 countries. The journal's compilers introduce *ASSIA* saying:

> *ASSIA* is aimed at meeting the information needs of all those who seek to serve people, be this in the social services, prison services, youth work, economics, politics, employment, race

relations etc. The sociological background to support the practice, however, is also included, hence *ASSIA* covers many of the major core journals in sociology.

Entries are listed alphabetically by subject. As with the indexing journals that I have looked at, *ASSIA* guides you from invalid to valid headings (e.g. 'SOCIAL STATUS *See* Elderly people: Social status'). It also indicates headings that are of related interest (e.g. 'SOCIAL STATUS *Related headings:* Peer status, Socioeconomic status'). Most of the headings are made up of a major keyword followed by one or more minor keywords. For example, I wanted to know what had been written recently about neighbourhoods. The most recent bimonthly issue of *ASSIA* available at the time included the information shown in Figure 2.13.

Notice that under the simple heading 'Neighbourhoods' you are directed to the heading 'Urban renewal: Neighbourhoods', but other entries follow in which the main heading 'Neighbourhoods' is associated with a number of other defining terms. The aim is to enable you to scan the list as quickly as possible to find an entry on that aspect of neighbourhoods which interests you most. So, for example, if you were interested in how the degree of cohe-

---

NEIGHBOURHOODS
    See
        Urban renewal: Neighbourhoods
NEIGHBOURHOODS: Cohesiveness: Measurement: Community psychology
The development of an instrument to measure neighbourhood cohesion. J.C. Buckner. *American Journal of Community Psychology*, 16 (Dec 88) p.771–91. *tbls*. <u>*refs*</u>.

The development of an instrument measuring a variable that represents a synthesis of the concepts of psychological sense of community, attraction-to-neighbourhood, and social interaction within a neighbourhood is reported. When this individual-level variable (termed "sense of community/cohesion") is assessed in a random sample of residents in a geographically bounded neighbourhood, the mean value forms a measure of the neighbourhood's cohesiveness. (*Abstract amended*)

NEIGHBOURHOODS: Satisfaction: Relationship with safety

Source: ASSIA, volume 3, number 3, 1989, p. 119.

Figure 2.13 Extract from *ASSIA*

siveness within a neighbourhood can be measured, the various keywords heading the Buckner entry would immediately attract your attention. The entry itself is in two sections: (1) the index part gives information about the article title, author and journal; and (2) the abstract provides a very short summary (only 64 words) of the main ideas of the paper, though enough to allow you to decide whether or not to spend time on obtaining a copy of the entire article.

Most abstracting journals specialise in particular discipline areas. They include: *Sociological Abstracts, Psychological Abstracts, International Political Science Abstracts, Abstracts in Anthropology, Geographical Abstracts, Historical Abstracts, Current Index to Journals in Education, Journal of Economic Literature, Social Work Research and Abstracts, Communication Abstracts, Family Studies Abstracts* (published by the Australian Institute of Family Studies), *Studies on Women Abstracts, Crime and Delinquency Abstracts, Sage Urban Studies Abstracts,* and *ANBAR* (a journal specialising in business studies). Bart and Frankel (1986, Chapter 5) list even more.

It will take you some time to become familiar with how to use abstracting journals, especially the major ones. Unfortunately, I have the space here to look in detail at only one. ***Sociological Abstracts***, the journal with which I am most familiar, is issued five times each year. There is also a cumulative annual index of authors, sources and subjects. However, the main body of the journal is not reissued as a single volume. Consequently, the annual index refers you to the five individual issues published during the year. Altogether, about 9000 abstracts of articles from over 700 journals are published annually. The abstracts are listed in 33 broad subject areas and 83 more specialised subject areas. For example, 'Mass Phenomena' is divided into seven smaller areas, including 'Social Movements', the 'Sociology of Leisure/Tourism', and the 'Sociology of Sports'.

To find articles on particular subjects you can use one of two methods. If your subject area is relatively broad (e.g. the sociology of crime) you can use the contents page at the front of each issue to find the page number for the start of the section. If, as is more likely, your subject area is more narrowly defined (e.g. suicide) you need to look at the subject index. For the most recent issues you will need to look in each one. For earlier issues, use the

SOCIOLOGICAL ABSTRACTS

annual cumulative subject index. The layout of the subject index is shown in Figure 2.14.

In the subject index a major heading (e.g. 'Suicide') is followed by several entries of other key words and phrases, each entry in the list starting on a new line and ending with a reference number. Again, the intention is to help you scan the list of articles (which can be several dozen entries long) to pinpoint those which are likely to be most useful. For example, if you are preparing an essay on suicide among teenagers you would follow up two of the entries in Figure 2.14: 'suicidal behavior, youths aged 12–16 . . . 89U6669'; and 'teenage suicide rates . . . 89U6673'. You need the reference numbers to find the journal abstracts in the main body of *Sociological Abstracts*. The first two numbers refer to the year an article was abstracted and the rest identifies its location within that year's list. The letter is always followed by four numbers, from 0001 to 9999. After reaching 9999 a new letter is assigned and the numbering system starts again at 0001.

You should have little difficulty in finding the abstract with a particular reference number if, as in this example, you're using the subject index of a single issue of *Sociological Abstracts* — that

---

Suicide
religion–suicide link, Emile Durkheim's theory, network approach; suicide
    rates; US counties; 89U5908
suicide–divorce relationship, Norway vs US; statistics; 89U6552
suicidal behavior, youths aged 12–16; psychiatric disorders, family
    dysfunction, parents' arrest rates; interview survey, 1983; 89U6669
suicidal target figures, male vs female reactions; scale ratings; vignettes;
    university undergraduates; 89U6689
suicide ideation, French-Canadians; stress/social support/personal
    characteristics; questionnaire survey; 89U6665
suicide incidence, dentists; occupational stress; interviews; 89U6133
suicide patterns, age/sex differences, USSR; questionnaire; Leningrad;
    1971–1982; 89U5699
suicide rates, Sri Lanka; internal migration; official statistics; 89U6671
suicide, definitional issue; 89U5728
suicide, reward system model vs conventional theories; cross-national
    data; 89U6667
suicide, social/legal policies, historical changes, Western civilization;
    demographic/other data; Biblical times–present; 89U6592
teenage suicide rates; television newscasts about suicide; national
    statistics; 1973–1984; 89U6673

Source: Sociological Abstracts, August 1989, p. 1199.

Figure 2.14 Extract from subject index of *Sociological Abstracts*

is, a recent issue not yet covered by a cumulated annual subject index. If you are using an annual index remember that it refers to five separate issues as there is no annual cumulation printed of the main body of *Sociological Abstracts*. If you do have a problem finding a particular abstract, turn to the contents pages which list both reference numbers and page numbers for each of the broad and narrow subject areas. Use the reference number of your article to identify the subject area it is in, and then check to see on which page this subject starts. It should then be easy to find the specific abstract. The layout of each entry in the main body of *Sociological Abstracts* is similar to that in *Applied Social Sciences Index and Abstracts* (see Figure 2.13), with information about the author (including a correspondence address), article and journal followed by an abstract of between 100 and 200 words.

Given the vast quantity of information available and the fairly mechanical task of searching for appropriate keywords, it is not surprising that **computer technology** is widely used to do literature searches. Basically, the information that you find in the printed copies of many indexing and abstracting journals is added to an electronic data base. Library users can then search for relevant information electronically rather than manually. If your library has an on-line public access catalogue (OPAC) you have probably already done some searching through an electronic data base.

There are two ways to get access to a data base containing information about journal articles: (1) you have the information on the data base sent to you on a compact disc; or (2) you link up to the data base using the telephone network. The first system uses **compact disc** technology (or CD-ROM). Tens of thousands of pages of text can be stored on one compact disc which can then be read by a personal computer. Many librarians see this method of storing and retrieving information as the face of the future in library services. Several indexing and abstracting journals, including *APAIS* (on the Austrom CD-ROM), *Sociological Abstracts* (called Sociofile) and *Psychological Abstracts* (PsycLit) are available on compact disc. With the CD-ROM system the library buys the compact discs and sets up a CD-ROM work station comprising a compact disc player, a personal computer and a printer. Readers use the computer to access the relevant information on the compact disc. They can then make a permanent copy of the results using the printer. It may well be that a CD-ROM work station is available to undergraduates in your library and that the library subscribes to a data base that is relevant to your course. If so, find out how to use the equipment — it will help you save a lot of time with your library searches.

The second way to access a data base is known as **on-line information retrieval** (or IR), and is similar to the OPAC system in many libraries. The data base is housed away from the library (possibly not even in Australia), and you access it using a computer and the telephone network. As most data bases are run as commercial operations, they charge a fee each time you do a search. According to Nancy Lane (1989, p. 108), 'Most searches cost between $50 and $75'. However, it is possible that all or part of the cost of an on-line search will be met by your library if the librarian considers that there are no suitable alternatives available. Generally, on-line information retrieval is used mainly by staff and postgraduate students. However, if later in your degree you have a particularly important project to complete and you don't find very much information using other methods, then it would be worthwhile asking at your library for details of their on-line information retrieval service.

Locating government reports

To operate efficiently government agencies need up-to-date, detailed information on a huge range of subjects. Governments, of course, are often in the unique position of being able to compel individuals and organisations to provide information; and governments are often the only organisations big enough to mount frequent, large-scale data collection exercises, whether it be a census or a massive enquiry into the deaths of Aboriginal prisoners in police custody. A large proportion of this information is published and available for general use.

You can **use official reports to help you write better essays**. For example, much of the statistical information in textbooks is out-of-date. This is not surprising considering that the authors have probably made use of published statistics when writing, and that it can take several years for a book to be written and published. In contrast, many government reports are published several times each year, providing statistics that are as up-to-date as possible. Moreover, the statistical information is often accompanied by commentaries which attempt to explain the figures. Occasionally, you will find that a government review of a particular social issue provides you with the most comprehensive source of background reading. For example, if you were examining health inequalities between major social groups in Australia (e.g. women/ men, middle class/working class, Aboriginals/non-Aboriginals) then one of the best places to start reading would be a chapter entitled 'Better health for all . . . not just for some' in the 1988 report *Health for All Australians* compiled for the Health Targets and Implementation (Health for All) Committee to Australian Health Ministers, and published by the Australian Government Publishing Service in Canberra. But you have to find it first!

As with the earlier sections on books and journal articles, I'll firstly make some comments about how to find the material included in a lecturer's reading list and then look in more detail at the more difficult problem of how to identify material to add to your own reading list.

Locating government reports from a reading list

The comments I made earlier about books in general also apply here. For example, if possible, do your catalogue search using the title of the report rather than the author's name. This is particularly useful advice when there is no specific person listed as author and the report is published under the name of a ministry, department, committee or other government body. When the name of the state or country is part of the name of the organisation then the author entry in the catalogue appears as you might expect (e.g. reports from the Australian Bureau of Agricultural and Resource Economics are catalogued under 'Australian Bureau of Agricultural and Resource Economics'). However, if the name of the government organisation does not indicate the relevant state or country, the author entry starts with the place name (e.g. reports from the Bureau of Industry Economics are catalogued under 'Australia. Bureau of Industry Economics').

Sometimes government reports from the same body but covering a wide range of topics are shelved together. For example, in my library all reports from the Australian Bureau of Statistics (ABS) are catalogued together in one part of the reference collection, filed by ABS catalogue number (about which I'll say more later). Similarly, there is an ongoing series called Parliamentary Papers, which include reports from Federal government departments, commissions of inquiry and various parliamentary committees. Each has a number, which is used when parliamentary papers are shelved. For example, Parliamentary Paper No. 2 of 1990, a Senate committee report on the pilots' strike, is shelved between Parliamentary Paper No. 1 of 1990, a Senate committee report of accommodation for disabled people, and Parliamentary Paper No. 3 of 1990, another Senate committee report, this one looking at pay for senior public servants.

Locating government reports without a reading list

There are two major reference tools to help you find government documents. The first is the *Australian National Bibliography (ANB)* which, as Figure 2.9 shows, indexes official reports as well as other Australian books. Recall that there is a subject index. More specific is **Australian Government Publications** *(AGP)*. A huge range of subjects are covered by *AGP* — the September 1990 subject list goes from 'AAEC' (the Australian Atomic Energy Commission) to 'Zucchini — Northern Territory'. To take one subject at random from this list, if you were preparing an essay on women working at home, you would find five entries under the subject heading 'Housewives' including, for example, a South Australian report, *Women in the Home* (Whitehorn 1989) and a Victorian report, *Women in the Home: It Was Nice To Be Asked* (Victorian Women's Consultative Council 1988).

Since 1988 *AGP* has been available only on microfiche and on-line. A microfiche copy is certainly less convenient to use than a printed copy, but it does have a couple of advantages. Firstly, each quarterly issue lists all previous publications for the year, which means that you don't have to wait for an annual cumulation. Secondly, the microfiche format allows the subject index to include a full reference for each publication, so you don't have to go from the subject index to the main body of the bibliography via a reference number.

Australian Bureau of Statistics

The Australian Bureau of Statistics (ABS) is the **official statistical organisation** for both federal and state governments. The amount

of data available from the ABS is indicated by the Bureau's size —
over $140 million were spent by the ABS during 1988–89, nearly
three-quarters of which went on salaries. In fact, the ABS has the
equivalent of over 3500 full-time staff. This many people can collect and collate an enormous volume of material. Altogether, the
ABS issues over 1500 reports annually under approximately 500
different titles (Australia, Parliament 1989). Of course, with this
much information made available each year, there is the very real
problem of not being able to see the wood for the trees. (Though
if the ABS were not around, a large number of trees might be!)

Although ABS publications are listed in the *Australian National
Bibliography* and *Australian Government Publications,* the easiest
way to track down an ABS report is to use the Bureau's own
Catalogue of Publications and Products (ABS 1990a). It is
published annually, and is free. (If you want to ask for a copy, the
address and telephone number of the ABS office in your state or
territory is in the telephone book, in the Commonwealth Government section at the start of the White Pages.) The *Catalogue* divides
ABS publications into the nine major groups listed in Figure 2.15.

Each ABS report has a **catalogue number**. For example, the
Catalogue of Publications and Products has the catalogue number
1101.0. The catalogue numbering scheme is simple to follow and
can be useful to know. The first digit refers to one of the groups
shown in Figure 2.15. Thus, the *Catalogue* (1101.0) is listed in the
'General' group. The second digit refers to a subgroup (e.g. the
General group is divided into: (1) 'Catalogues and Guides'; (2)
'Manuals'; and (3) 'Yearbooks'). Thus, the *Catalogue* (1101.0) is
listed in the 'Catalogues and Guides' subgroup. The next two dig-

---

1. General (including yearbooks)
2. Census of Population and Housing
3. Demography (i.e. population statistics)
4. Social statistics (including education, health, welfare and justice)
5. National accounts; finance and foreign trade
6. Labour statistics and prices
7. Agriculture (including fishing)
8. Secondary industry and distribution (including mining and building)
9. Transport

Source: ABS 1990a.

Figure 2.15   Major groups of ABS publications

its refer to the location of the report within the subgroup (e.g. 01 is the first report in the subgroup, 50 is the fiftieth report in the subgroup). Thus, the *Catalogue* (11<u>01</u>.0) is the first one listed under 'Catalogues and Guides'. The final digit, after the decimal point, shows the office issuing the report. It usually also indicates the geographical area covered (e.g. 0 is Australia, 1 is NSW, 2 is Victoria). Thus, the *Catalogue* (1101.<u>0</u>) is an Australia-wide report. Because of the large number of ABS publications, you should always give the catalogue number when referring to a report put out by the ABS.

By far the most generally useful of all ABS publications are the **Australian and state yearbooks**. Each is a mine of statistical information with tables, diagrams and written commentaries. The 1990 edition of *Year Book Australia* (catalogue number 1301.0) runs to 846 pages and has entries on everything from 'AAT' (check it out) to 'Zinc'. Moreover, these yearbooks are usually to be found in the reference section of the smallest public library so that even isolated off-campus students should have fairly ready access to them.

Census of Population and Housing Undoubtedly the biggest and best-known of the many surveys conducted by the ABS is the Census of Population and Housing — the one survey which, as far as possible, includes everybody in Australia. I'll illustrate the **size of the census operation** (most appropriately) with a few figures. According to the Bureau's *Annual Report* for 1986–87 (Australia, Parliament 1987) the collection and computer entry of the 1986 census data cost nearly $45 million. Much of this money was spent employing 25 000 people to hand out and collect the census forms and 1200 people to prepare and enter the results for computer analysis. You can find background information about the census in the series of Census Information Papers, the most generally useful of which is *How Australia Takes a Census* (2176.0).

A census has been taken every five years in Australia since 1961. Earlier censuses, taken at irregular intervals, go back to 1911. **Each census is slightly different** as topics are added and deleted and questions about on-going topics are modified. Figure 2.16 shows topics covered by the 1986 census.

PERSONS

1. Name
2. Sex
3. Age
4. Relationship to householder
5. Marital status (e.g. never married/married)
6. Usual address
7. Usual address 1 year ago
8. Usual address 5 years ago
9. Aboriginal or Torres Strait Islander (Yes/No)
10. Country of birth
11. Year of arrival in Australia
12. Father's country of birth
13. Mother's country of birth
14. Australian citizen (Yes/No)
15. Ancestry (e.g. Greek/English/Indian)
16. Religious denomination
17. Language other than English used at home
18. Fluency in English (e.g. very well/well)
19. Attending an educational institution (Yes/No) + Type (e.g. pre-school)
20. Year first married
21. Married more than once (Yes/No)
22. Age left school
23. Post-school qualifications
24. Gross annual income (e.g. $15,001–$18,000)
25. If woman, how many babies
26. In full-time or part-time work last week (e.g. yes, paid work)
27. Looked for work in last month (Yes/No)
28. Type job last week (e.g. wage/salary earner)
29. Type of occupation last week (e.g. coal miner)
30. Main tasks in that occupation
31. Employer (name and address)
32. Kind of industry carried out by employer (e.g. dairy farming)
33. Hours worked in main job last week
34. Mode of transport to work today (e.g. tram)

DWELLINGS

H1. Number of each type of room
H2. Number of motor vehicles
H3. Dwelling rented or owned:
   If rented: landlord, weekly rent, un/furnished
   If owned: bought or mortgaged; mortgage repayments
H4. Details of people usually resident, but absent on census night (name, sex, age, relationship to householder, marital status, full-time student)

Source: ABS 1986a.

Figure 2.16 Topics covered in the 1986 census

Individuals' answers to the questions asked about each topic in Figure 2.16 are grouped together at a **number of geographical scales**. Some of them are shown in Figure 2.17. The basic building block is the collection district (CD), each containing 200–300 households. CDs are joined to form a local government area (LGA) — the area administered by a local council (e.g. I live in one of 34 CDs making up the LGA). LGAs are joined to form a statistical division (SD) which is a regional area, often focused socially and economically on a central town or city (e.g. my LGA is one of 16 making up the SD). The next geographical level is the state (e.g. my SD is one of 12 within Victoria). And finally, of course, information from the six states and two territories are combined to produce national data.

When you combine the range of possible topics (see Figure 2.16) with the range of geographical scales (see Figure 2.17) you end up with a **huge mass of data**. Questions ranging from the very general 'How many men and women are there in Australia?' to the very specific 'How many single men (or women) aged 18 to 22

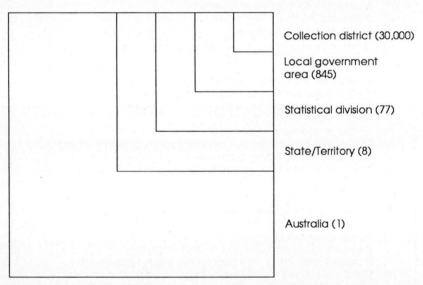

Collection district (30,000)

Local government area (845)

Statistical division (77)

State/Territory (8)

Australia (1)

Note: The figures in brackets show the number of areas at each geographical level in 1986.
Source: ABS 1986b and 1987.

Figure 2.17 Some geographical scales at which census information is available

live in my collection district?' can all be answered using information from the census. The more general the question the more likely it is that an answer will be readily available.

If you are a first-year undergraduate, you are most likely to want information about **single characteristics at the national or state level**. At the national level, the '1986 Census Reports' series (2501.0 to 2522.0) covers a wide range of topics, from the very general *Australia in Profile* (2502.0) to the very specific *Australia's Caravan Park Dwellers* (2509.0). At the state level there are two sets of reports, both with catchy titles: *Summary Characteristics of Persons and Dwellings* (2479.0 to 2487.0) and *Cross-classified Characteristics of Persons and Dwellings* (2490.0 to 2498.0). In the first set, each table shows only one characteristic so that, for example, you can check the number of men and women or the number of people in each age group. In the second set of reports, each table cross-classifies (or cross-tabulates) two characteristics so that, for example, you can check the number of men and women in each age group. (Both series also have a report covering Australia as a whole.) In addition, each state and territory office of the ABS produces special reports based on the 1986 census (2201.1 to 2501.8). Check the *Catalogue* for details.

At the **local government area level** the main series of printed reports is *Profile of Legal Local Government Areas — Usual Resident Counts* (2470.0 to 2476.0). Only sixteen of the topics listed in Figure 2.16 are covered and there is no cross-classifying of topics. Similar reports are available for the Australian Capital Territory (2477.0) and Brisbane (2478.0). Both places are divided into statistical local areas because of the absence of suitably-sized legal LGAs.

Not surprisingly, there are no printed reports for the 30 000 or so **collection districts**, though information is available on microfiche (as it is for all geographical levels). It is important, of course, to identify exactly which CDs you are interested in. Ask for advice at your library or telephone the ABS information service in your capital city. All levels of 1986 census data, including collection districts, are also available on a CD-ROM package called CDATA. With it you can produce tables and maps for virtually all the topics covered by the 1986 census. Your library may have a copy.

Other ABS Surveys Although the biggest survey the census is by no means the only one carried out by the ABS, as the subject

index in its catalogue indicates. I'll illustrate how you can use the
ABS *Catalogue* to track down some results from one of these other
ABS surveys. Imagine that you are writing an essay on job mobility, or how often people change jobs. One of the sections will
examine whether people's job mobility is related to the sort of
work they do. In other words, do people in different occupations
have different job mobility patterns? If possible, you want some
up-to-date Australian data to help you answer this question.

Job mobility is one of the headings in the subject index of the
1990 ABS *Catalogue*. (Often, of course, your first subject heading
may not be listed and you'll need to search for alternative headings.)
The 'Job Mobility' entry is as follows, with each catalogue number
followed by a page number in brackets: 6206.2 (131); 6208.0 (123);
6209.0 (123); 6209.1 (130). Recall that the number after the decimal
point shows which ABS office has published the report (e.g. 0 is
Australia, 1 is NSW, 2 is Victoria). The job mobility list thus includes two national reports (6208.0 and 6209.0), one from NSW
(6209.1) and one from Victoria (6206.2). As you want national job
mobility figures, you can narrow down the search to the two national

HAVE A GLANCE THROUGH OUR
CATALOGUE ~ YOU *MAY* FIND A
SURVEY THAT REALLY GRABS YOU

ABS

reports. The subject entry shows that both are listed on page 123 in the main body of the *Catalogue* (6208.0 (123), 6209.0 (123)). Figure 2.18 shows how the two reports are described.

The *Catalogue* entry for 6209.0 shows that the *Labour Mobility, Australia* report includes tables on the two characteristics of interest to you — labour mobility and occupation. To find out whether, for example, managers change jobs more or less often than labourers, you need a cross-classification of labour mobility by occupation. The *Catalogue* doesn't say exactly what cross-classification tables are included in the report. You need to find the *Labour Mobility, Australia* report itself. It is likely that all ABS materials are shelved together in your library, probably by catalogue number. If ABS reports are not mentioned in the various library guides ask a member of the library staff where they are shelved.

The *Catalogue* entry shows that *Labour Mobility, Australia* is an annual publication. Make sure that you look at the most recent edition — remember that the aim of the exercise is to use information which is as up-to-date as possible. The contents page of the 1990 edition (the most recent available at the time) lists Table 9 as 'Persons who were working in February 1990; duration of

---

6208.0   Labour Mobility, Australia, Summary

Annual; first issue: November 1972; 10pp; $5.00

Previously: Labour Mobility, Australia, Preliminary

Contains estimates covering selected aspects of the survey. For full details *see* 6209.0.

6209.0   Labour Mobility, Australia

Annual; first issue: November 1972; 24pp; $8.00

Estimates of persons who worked at some time during the year ending February, employed for less than twelve months in job held at the end of the period, left a job in the period. Classifications are: number of employers or businesses in the period, sex, age, industry, occupation, educational attainment, marital status, status of worker, labour mobility, change in occupation and industry, duration of job left.

Source: ABS 1990a, p. 123. Commonwealth of Australia copyright reproduced by permission.

Figure 2.18   Extract from the ABS *Catalogue*

current job and occupation'. This is exactly what you need. Part of the ABS table is shown in Table 2.1. As it stands, the table does not provide you with an instant answer to your research question, but you have the information to work on.

Table 2.1   Persons in work: duration of current job by occupation (Australia, February 1990)

Duration of current job (years)	Managers and administrators ('000s)	Labourers and related workers ('000s)
Under 1	119	373
1 to less than 2	73	179
2 to less than 3	72	117
3 to less than 5	109	153
5 to less than 10	157	177
10 to less than 20	158	156
20 and over	162	58
Total	850	1212

Source: Based on ABS 1990b, Table 9.

Further reading

This chapter gives you enough general advice to allow you to develop your library skills using the catalogue in your own library, *ANB, APAIS,* relevant abstracting journals, the ABS *Catalogue,* and so on. However, if you need more information you may find the following book useful:

Lane, N.D. 1989, *Techniques for Student Research: A Practical Guide*, Longman Cheshire, Melbourne.

There are a number of library skills books written for specific disciplines. They are intended primarily for postgraduate and senior undergraduate students. They include:

Bart, P. & Frankel, L. 1986, *The Student Sociologist's Handbook*, 4th edn, Random House, New York.

Read, J.G. & Baxter, P.M. 1983, *Library Use: A Handbook for Psychology,* American Psychological Association, Washington, DC.

In the following paperback Martin Slattery discusses how valid official statistics really are. He provides an excellent introduction to the radical critique of official statistics — that all governments collect the minimum number of potentially embarrassing statistics, either by not providing the money to collect them or by making sure that the concepts being surveyed are measured in such a way as to do the least political damage:

Slattery, M. 1986, *Official Statistics,* Tavistock, London.

STATISTICS BUREAU OF EASILY
EMBARRASSED GOVERNMENT

3

Writing skills

Introduction

During your degree program you are likely to complete about 50 written assignments, totalling approximately 100 000 words — almost twice the length of this book. If you spend an average of 20 hours per assignment, this writing will take you 1000 hours. The basic aim of this chapter is to help make sure that you expend all this time and effort as productively as possible!

Before looking in detail at how to write a good essay I'll briefly explain why there is such a heavy reliance on written work in your course. Firstly, **from your lecturer's point of view written assignments have several advantages** over other forms of assessment. Papers are portable and largely impersonal. They can be marked in different places at different times at the convenience of the marker (as indicated by the mysterious stains that sometimes appear on essays). Written papers, especially those which have been typed or word processed, can be looked at objectively — as stand-alone works separate from their authors. Authors, of course, have their own personalities and habits, some of which may or may not endear them to the marker! Obviously, markers always strenuously try to avoid letting personal sympathies and antagonisms influence their judgement of students' work, but it is certainly easier to do this when dealing with a disembodied essay than when judging a personal presentation in a tutorial. Moreover, it is easier to moderate written work. In other words, it is easier for someone unconnected with the teaching of the course (the moderator) to judge whether a student's work has been assessed fairly.

Secondly, the preparation of written reports is a **crucial skill**

needed for many jobs taken up by social science and humanities graduates. As society in general, and work organisations in particular, become more complex, the ability to write a logically argued report, backed up by strong evidence and presented in clear and concise terms, becomes increasingly important. Also highly valued is the skill to write such a report in the limited time available — deadlines are important both in higher education and in the workplace.

Thirdly, and most importantly, essay writing helps you to **develop your intellectual abilities**. In other words, essay writing forces you to think! You have to develop your skills of analysis and synthesis — to break down a complex idea or argument into smaller, more manageable and understandable parts (analysis), and then to put these together to form your own logically structured, well-written account (synthesis). Reading someone else's logically structured, well-written paper may take a large amount of perspiration, but it usually requires relatively little inspiration. Writing your own logically structured, well-written paper is likely to take large amounts of both perspiration and inspiration.

Often, **essay writing forces you to think about the same issue from several points of view**. You may be asked to explain a social phenomenon from more than one perspective and then to weigh up, or evaluate, the evidence to see which perspective has the strongest arguments. This process of presenting the evidence (i.e. being counsel for both the prosecution and the defence) and then weighing it up and giving a verdict (i.e. being both judge and jury) is crucial to intellectual development. It helps you avoid looking at issues in a blinkered way. Instead, it encourages you to judge the evidence on its merits. Sometimes you end up changing your mind about a particular issue. For example, I carried out some major research into public participation in the local environmental planning process (Burdess 1986a). I was a strong supporter of the idea of public participation at the start of the research, but by the end I was very sceptical of its value — at least in the ways it was organised by the planning profession.

There is a wide variety of written assignments. A major division is between **library research and original research**. Most undergraduate work is library-based research — that is, based on books and journals to be found in the university or college library. You may also be required to do original research, collecting new data by survey, laboratory or field work. However, this sort of research tends to come in the later stages of a degree program. Consequently, in this introductory text I'll concentrate on how to write papers based on library research.

Library research papers themselves can vary. Figure 3.1 shows three types — abstracts, reviews and essays. As you can see, they vary in terms of the level of evaluation and the range of literature used. Thus, an abstract describes only one piece of work, usually a journal article. A review not only describes one piece of work, usually a book, but also evaluates how far it clarifies and extends the material in other related books. An essay is usually concerned with some general social issue or idea which is described (in brief) and evaluated (in detail) using a wide variety of literary sources. I'll look briefly at abstracts and book reviews, and then I'll examine in more detail the most common form of assessment — the essay.

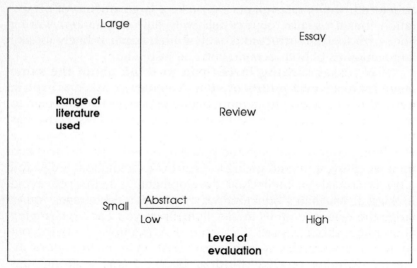

Figure 3.1   Types of library research papers

Abstracts

You will be familiar with abstracts if you have looked at any of the leading journals in your subject area, or if you have used any of the abstracting journals mentioned in Chapter 2. In no more than 500 words (usually less) an abstract describes the most important points — the bare bones — of an article that may run to several thousand words. **An abstract is descriptive, not evaluative**: it summarises the research — it does not judge how well it was done. An effective summary is not simply a list of headings. For example, the following is not an effective summary of a lengthy description of someone's physical appearance: 'The person is described in terms of sex, age, height, weight, facial features, hairstyle and clothing'. Similarly, the following is not an effective summary of a lengthy journal article: 'The paper outlines the basic hypotheses, reviews the relevant literature, reports the results, and ends with some very interesting conclusions'. These 'summaries' leave you completely in the dark about the person and the paper.

An abstract clearly refers to just one piece of work and is intended to provide the maximum amount of information in the minimum number of words. Consequently, it is unnecessary to start each sentence with phrases such as 'The paper notes' or 'The author maintains'. An abstract is the *only* piece of work where you don't have to use quotation marks around text which appears in the original — it is assumed that the abstract will contain much of the author's own material.

Book reviews

A second type of written assignment based on library research is a book review. Once again, you will be familiar with book reviews if you have looked at any of the leading journals in your subject area, or if you have used any of the specialised indexes of book reviews such as *Book Review Digest*. Reviews are more wide-ranging than abstracts, often comparing the reviewed book with others in the same field, and including evaluation as well as description. Even so, reviews are usually less than 1000 words in length.

The role of a book reviewer is similar to that of an essay marker — a review of a book is an extended version of a marker's commentary on the structure, style and layout of an essay. Consequently, much of the material on essay writing in the remaining sections of this chapter will be helpful when you have to write a book review. In this section I'll simply highlight the most important general issues.

The first task of an essay marker is to get a clear idea of the exact question the essay is designed to answer, as it is only then that the marker can begin to judge how well the essay is doing its job. Similarly, it is important to be clear about the exact **purpose of the book** you're reviewing. The title and subtitle should, of course, give some clues, but you are likely to find a more extended rationale for the book on the back cover or in an introductory section of the book. It's useful to include this information near the start of your review so that your readers are immediately clear about the basic purpose of the book. It might also be useful to say whether any other books have a similar purpose so that later, if necessary, you can make comparisons of the structure, style and layout of each.

Most of the review is likely to be taken up with a discussion of the **structure of the book** — that is, the topics covered and how they are organised. Bear in mind that the person reading your review may know little or nothing about the book itself. Consequently, you need to describe the structure of the book. For example, with *The Handbook of Student Skills*, you would firstly mention the three main sections — study skills, library skills and writing skills — and then give a thumbnail sketch of each (e.g. in the section on study skills, a before–during–after chronological sequence is used when discussing the various types of class work and exams). The descriptive section is usually followed by an evaluation of the book's structure. Ask yourself if the structure can be improved. Are chapters or sections included that really should be left out? Are chapters or sections left out that really should be included? Are the relevant chapters or sections in the most appropriate order and, if not, how can the order be improved?

Two much shorter sections in your review might deal with **writing style and book layout**. With regard to writing style, the main issue will probably be whether or not the level of formality of the writing is appropriate for the likely readership. For example, a general introductory textbook like *The Handbook of Student Skills* should be written in a different style to a very specialised text on social theory. However, even advanced texts should be intelligible to students specialising in the area. If you read a paragraph several times without being able to understand it, it is likely that the author's style needs improving! Illustrate any writing problems with a well-chosen quotation (inside quotation marks, with the relevant page number in brackets). You might also want to comment briefly on aspects of the book layout such as the adequacy of the contents and index pages, the use of headings and different typefaces, and the quality and quantity of illustrative materials — tables, diagrams and photographs.

Finally, you need to give some **overall conclusion** about the book. Remind your readers of the basic purpose of the book, and say to what degree the author has succeeded in doing what he or she set out to do. Overall, give your opinion as to whether or not the book is a useful addition to the existing literature in the area.

I have looked only briefly at abstracts and reviews because most of the time you will be asked to write essays. These tend to be longer than either reviews or abstracts (averaging about 2000 words) and, as Figure 3.1 indicates, they are generally the most wide-ranging and evaluative type of paper. In the next few sections I'll look in some detail at how to go about planning and writing an essay.

Planning an essay

An essay is like a house — each is an entity in itself, but made up of a number of interconnected parts. Deciding what rooms there should be and where they should go is a major part of the house design process. Similarly, deciding on the sections of the essay and how they should be ordered is a major part of the essay planning process. This planning process can be broken into two major sequences: first, identifying the basic structure of the essay; and second, developing this basic structure into a more detailed blueprint. I'll look at each in turn.

Basic essay plan

I'll assume that you have a fairly limited knowledge of your essay topic and that your lecturer has directed you to a handful of key references. In preparation for the essay you have collected together your own copy of each of the key references and you are ready to start planning the essay. This early period is always the most difficult and daunting. In front of you is a small pile of probably unread book chapters and journal articles and a notepad containing only the essay title. The aim of the session is to draw up the first draft of your basic essay plan — the skeleton of your eventual essay.

You are immediately confronted with a chicken-and-egg problem. The idea is to draw up an essay plan so that when you read the literature you take notes only on those issues that will be included in the essay. Of course, you can't decide on the essay plan until you know what are the important points and how they fit together. Unfortunately, often you can't identify the important points until you have read the literature!

As time is usually short, the temptation is to move as quickly as possible onto the note-making part of the essay writing process. Note-making produces concrete results — you can see what you've done. In contrast, planning the structure of the essay can seem relatively unproductive — you can spend a long time producing a plan consisting of only a couple of dozen words. Nevertheless, they will be the couple of dozen words on which the entire essay will hang. Consequently, **this planning stage is the most important one**. It shouldn't be rushed through to get to what are more physically active but intellectually less important stages. There are three stages to developing the basic essay plan: (1) brainstorming the essay question; (2) analysing the literature; and (3) ordering the essay sections. I'll look at each in turn.

Brainstorming the essay question

The first step is to **define exactly what it is that you are being asked to do**. Look at the essay title carefully — word by word. You obviously need a clear understanding of each word or phrase in the question. Check unfamiliar technical words (alienation? patriarchy? molar environment?) in a specialist subject dictionary. The more specialised your course the more useful it is to own a subject dictionary. Sometimes unfamiliar non-technical words or phrases may also need to be looked up (dissipate? heterogeneous? Pyrrhic victory?). Make sure that you have your own general dictionary so you can check any unfamiliar words. However, bear in mind that it is often the *familiar* words that determine the nature of an essay. For example, 'What role does government play in the Australian economy?' is a very different question from the similar sounding 'What role should government play in the Australian economy?'

Often an essay title can be simplified to the phrase 'Do this'. Thus, you first need to identify the commanding verb which tells you what to do. For example, you may be required to compare, consider, contrast, describe, evaluate, explain, illustrate, interpret, outline, review, or summarise. You then need to identify what it is that you have to compare, consider, contrast, etc. Sometimes the question asks you to look at just one thing (e.g. 'Describe the Westminster system of government'). Sometimes you may be asked to look at two (or more) things (e.g. 'Compare the Westminster and Washington systems of government'). One of the major tasks of the brainstorming session is to work out whether you have to write an essay focusing on one thing, or an essay comparing two or more things (i.e. a comparative essay).

Unfortunately, the need to write a **comparative essay** is not always so clearly highlighted as it is in the above example! Consider the following question, which I'll use as an ongoing example in the following pages: 'Why are there varying rates of illness between social classes?' Try to find the commanding verb. It's not easy as it is only implied in the question wording. You are being asked to *explain* something. There's just one thing to explain — the varying rates of illness between social classes. Thus, at first glance it doesn't seem that a comparative essay is needed. However, within the social sciences and humanities there are often different explanations about why things occur. Thus, if you're asked to explain something, the chances are you will have a number of different explanations to choose from. Often, the best thing to do is to write a comparative essay — an essay comparing the different explanations or arguments. Essays such as this are often asked for. If the essay question, either explicitly or implicitly, asks you to explain, interpret or evaluate, it often means that you will have to write a comparative essay.

Thus, if the essay title indicates that you need to write a comparative essay, you may be able to fill in the headings of the columns of your basic essay plan. For example, if you're asked to compare the Westminster and Washington systems of government, your two column headings are self-defined. If you are asked to explain the varying rates of illness between social classes, you might have a feeling that a comparative essay is required. You would therefore look out for competing explanations when you start to read through the literature.

Usually it's useful to **describe** something before explaining it.

Thus, before explaining the varying rates of illness between social classes, it's important to say exactly what these varying rates of illness are. Consequently, one of the early sections of the essay will need to describe how the rates of illness vary between social classes. But it will be a relatively short section, setting the scene for the later explanations.

What about **time and space parameters** — should the essay refer to a particular time and/or to a particular place? The present tense of the verb in the class and illness question ('Why *are* there . . .') indicates that, as far as possible, you should explain present-day variations in the rates of illness. But there is no reference to a particular place. You therefore need to define your geographical area of interest. You will probably need to focus on particular areas. Much will depend on the places looked at by your key authors. However, it seems unlikely that, for example, the social pattern of illness in Australia will be markedly different from that in Britain or North America. It is something you need to bear in mind when you start reading through the literature.

You might also wonder about the **direction of the association** between illness and class. Does class determine illness, or does illness determine class? For example, if members of the working class have a higher level of illness than members of the middle class, is this because there is something about being working class that causes higher levels of illness (i.e. class $\rightarrow$ illness), or is it because illness results in people being able to hold down only working class jobs (i.e. illness $\rightarrow$ class)? Common sense might suggest that the class $\rightarrow$ illness model is more likely to be correct — a coal miner getting a lung disease seems somewhat more likely than a man becoming a labourer because he wasn't fit enough to become a managing director.

Points such as these might go through your head in the initial brainstorming session. None of them are the result of any specialised knowledge about illness and social class. It's possible that some will be incorrect and will have to be discarded. However, at this early stage all are worth bearing in mind — and jotting them down helps you to bear them in mind. Having done some brainstorming the next stage is to see what the literature has to say.

Analysing the literature
To start, simply browse through the literature you've collected

and identify the parts that seem most relevant to your essay topic. You will certainly need to use the contents page in the front of each book, and possibly the index pages at the back. The abstract and the section headings of each of the journal articles will also be useful. Then, for each book and article take a fresh sheet of notepaper and write the author's surname and the date of publication on the top. You should already have the full reference on a catalogue card (see Figure 2.7). The aim now is to **recreate each original author's outline plan** — that is, to produce a series of headings, subheadings and paragraph themes for each article and chapter.

To prepare these outlines, **you do not need to read each of your key references in great detail**. It is likely that each author has a series of headings and probably subheadings. If so, your main task is to identify the paragraph themes. A common writing practice is to start each paragraph with a key sentence that summarises the basic point raised in the rest of the paragraph. If this is the case, there is no need to read further than the first sentence in each paragraph when compiling your outline plan. If the first one or two sentences don't give you the paragraph theme, look at the last sentence in the paragraph, as another common writing practice is to summarise the current paragraph before moving onto the next one. In addition, important words are often highlighted by bold type or italics. As you list the headings, subheadings and paragraph themes, make sure that you make a note in the margin of the page numbers. They will be extremely useful later when you begin to read the key references in more detail.

After looking through your four or five key references you should be able to spread out the four or five pages of outline notes, and begin to draw up the first draft of your basic essay plan. You are looking for two things — comparative groups and analytical categories. I'll look at each in turn.

Comparative groups I said earlier that you often have to write comparative essays. **You might be asked to compare different time periods, geographical areas, social groups, or social theories.** The need for a comparative essay may be explicit in the essay title (e.g. 'Compare the Westminster and Washington systems of government'). If this is the case, you will have identified the comparative groups in the initial brainstorming session. On the other hand, the need for a comparative essay may be buried within the essay question (e.g. 'Why are there varying rates of illness between social classes?'). In this case, the key references should make clear that you need to write a comparative essay. For example, in the class and illness essay you are likely to end up comparing conservative and radical arguments about varying rates of illness between social classes. The radical explanation of the higher rate of illness among the working class population is that the capitalist system of production is inherently harmful to the health of its workers. As there is a basic conflict between profits and health, a healthy society can come about only after a complete restructuring of the capitalist system. In contrast, conservatives explain the high levels of illness among working class people by their misuse of the freedoms and prosperity that the capitalist system has provided — that 'carelessness, gluttony, drunkenness, and sloth take some of their wages in illness' (Kass 1975, p. 31). The conservative view is not to change the system but for working class people to change their behaviour. Thus, the radical explanation and the conservative explanation are the two comparative groups that you would use in this essay.

Analytical categories Regardless of whether or not you're asked to write a comparative essay, your main planning task is to identify some analytical categories. In other words, you need to break down the large and complex subject area which is the focus of the essay title into several smaller and simpler categories. Often your literature search will produce a **ready-made series of analytical categories**. For example, a system of government can be divided into three parts: the legislature (e.g. parliament and congress); the executive (e.g. prime minister and president); and the judiciary (e.g. judges and lawyers). Similarly, the complex concept of culture can be looked at in terms of mentifacts (e.g. language and religion), sociofacts (e.g. family and school), and artifacts (e.g. food and clothing). Finally, the role that a person plays at work can be analysed in terms of the influence of external factors (e.g. organisational structure and administration) and the influence of internal factors (e.g. personal values and education).

Alternatively, a complex issue may be broken down by using a number of **historical periods**. For example, an essay on postwar Australian immigration can be divided into three periods: a period of assimilation; a period of integration; and the current period of multiculturalism. The three periods mark the historical trend of an increasing recognition that traditional Australian society would change as a result of immigration (Bates and Linder-Pelz 1990, p. 30). Or possibly a **geographical perspective** might be useful in identifying analytical categories. For example, in a paper on social change in rural England, I firstly look at changes that have taken place on the farm, such as the transformation of agriculture into agribusiness; then at changes in the village, such as the influx of people from the cities; and finally at changes at the district or regional level, such as the party politicisation of local government (Burdess 1986b).

Sometimes analytical categories are the product of **combining two characteristics**, or dimensions, of an issue. In Chapter 1, for example, I look at the various roles that students often take in tutorials. I define four types of role by combining what I think are two important dimensions — whether or not students prepare for the tutorials, and whether or not students participate in tutorials. The combination of the two preparation categories and the two participation categories produce four distinctive types of tutorial role (see Figure 1.2). Notice that in this example I divide each characteristic as simply as possible — students either do or do not prepare, and either do or do not participate. Of course, there is a large range of possible levels of both preparation and participation. These can be shown by using a graph rather than a table when trying to identify analytical categories. I use a graphing technique in the introduction to this chapter when identifying types of written work (see Figure 3.1). Again, I pick out what I believe are two important characteristics — the range of literature used to prepare the work, and the degree of evaluation contained in the work. I plot these as the two sides of a graph and then identify three types of written work on the graph.

Rather than giving more brief illustrations of analytical categories, I'll go back to an earlier example and look in detail at the **development of the social class and illness essay**. Recall that the question requires a comparative essay — you need to compare conservative and radical explanations of the different rates of illness between social classes. So far, however, I have not identified any analytical categories. When looking at the literature on rates of illness between social classes I found that much of the radical literature emphasises work-related issues, such as exposure to dangerous work practices and industrial chemicals. In contrast, much of the conservative literature emphasises home-related issues, such as smoking and diet. More generally, the radical literature

Analytical categories	Comparative groups	
	Radical	Conservative
Production	✔	✔
Consumption	✔	✔

Figure 3.2 Major sections for the main body of the social class and illness essay

looks mainly at the production process while the conservative literature looks mainly at the consumption process. Production and consumption can thus become the two major analytical categories in the essay. Combining the two comparative groups (radical and conservative) and the two analytical categories (production and consumption) produces four main sections for inclusion in the main body of the essay, as shown in Figure 3.2.

Like most simple devices, once you've worked it out you wonder how on earth it could have taken you so long to think of it. But **the basic structure usually comes after some long, hard thinking**, trying a number of alternatives before coming up with something which you think might work. Sometimes you end up with a structure that leaves you with a nagging feeling that something is not quite right. If so, don't forget that this is only your first draft and whatever it is that's troubling you is likely to become clearer later on, allowing you to make any necessary changes to the basic essay plan.

Ordering the essay sections

Once you have identified the main sections of your essay you have to decide on the order in which you will discuss them. Generally in a comparative essay, regardless of whether you're comparing arguments, groups, times or places, it is advisable to **deal with each analytical category in turn** — firstly with regard to one argument, group, time or place, and then with the other. In this way you make a more direct point-by-point comparison. Thus, in the class and illness essay, it is better to look at both sets of arguments about the production process, followed by both sets of arguments about the consumption process.

It seems logical to consider production first and consumption later, goods needing to be produced before they can be consumed. But what is the best way of ordering the conservative and radical arguments for each of the analytical categories? The four options are shown in Figure 3.3.

What is needed is the **least biased and most logical order**. Always presenting one set of arguments first (options 1 and 2) might bias the essay. For example, if radical views always precede conservative views (option 2) it could result in an essay which is seen to be biased towards the radical viewpoint. Alternating the sequence so that one set of arguments is dealt with first in one half, and the second in the other half (options 3 and 4) would result in a more even-handed structure. Recall that the radical literature stresses the production process and the conservative literature stresses the consumption process. To a large degree, what the conservatives say about the production process is a response to what the radicals say about production, and what the radicals say about the consumption process is a response to what the conservatives say about consumption. As it is logical to present argument followed by counter-argument, the most balanced and logical sequence of sections is thus option 4 — that is, (1) radical views of the production process, (2) conservative views of the production process, (3) conservative views of the consumption process, and (4) radical views of the consumption process.

These four sections, explaining variations in illness between social classes, will form the bulk of the essay. In addition, remem-

Option 1	Option 2
1. Conservative–production	1. Radical–production
2. Radical–production	2. Conservative–production
3. Conservative–consumption	3. Radical–consumption
4. Radical–consumption	4. Conservative–consumption
Option 3	**Option 4**
1. Conservative–production	1. Radical–production
2. Radical–production	2. Conservative–production
3. Radical–consumption	3. Conservative–consumption
4. Conservative–consumption	4. Radical–consumption

Figure 3.3 Options for ordering major sections in the social class and illness essay

ber that you usually need to describe something before you can adequately explain it (an idea first raised during the initial brainstorming session). Consequently, a short descriptive section is also needed to show exactly how illness rates vary between social classes. In addition, an introductory section and a concluding section are likely to be useful. (I'll say more about these later.) Overall, therefore, this initial planning stage has produced the basic essay plan shown in Figure 3.4.

---

1. Introduction

2. Describing variations in illness between social classes

3. Explaining variations in illness between social classes
    3.1 Radical arguments about the production process
    3.2 Conservative counter-arguments about the production process
    3.3 Conservative arguments about the consumption process
    3.4 Radical counter-arguments about the consumption process

4. Conclusion

Figure 3.4 Social class and illness: basic essay plan

WELL BALANCED RADICAL & CONSERVATIVE ESSAYS

Detailed essay plan

It is only after you have worked out the basic essay plan that you can start thinking about reading the literature more carefully. This is because your reading can now focus on the issues shown in the headings of your basic essay plan. For example, with the class and illness essay, you can look specifically for material that describes variations in illness between social classes, and, more especially, material that outlines radical and conservative explanations of these variations in terms of the production and consumption processes.

One of the major differences between essay writing at secondary and tertiary levels is the **much wider range of reading** expected of tertiary students. For example, a couple of textbooks plus class notes could well be sufficient at high school, while use of a dozen sources would not be unusual at college or university, even at first-year level. The wider the range of literature the more difficult it is to remember who said what, where and when. Notes are the bridge between other people's writing and your own. They aren't an optional extra. Notes are essential if you are to make the most of the facts and ideas you come across in your reading.

I use a **two-stage approach to note-taking**. It involves: (1) compiling author notes — that is, notes on what each author says about all the basic sections of the essay plan; and (2) compiling section notes — that is, notes on what all authors say about each of the basic sections of the essay plan (see Figure 3.5). I'll deal with each in turn.

Author notes

You now begin to look in some detail at your four or five key references to **see what each author says about your essay topic**. Once again, you need a new sheet of A4-sized paper for each source, with the author and date at the top. You can use

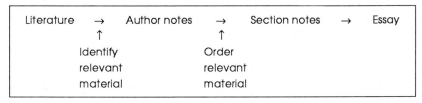

Figure 3.5 Author notes and section notes

your existing very brief notes to locate those pages you need to take notes from. Note down information which you think will be relevant in any of the sections shown in the basic essay plan. Start each point on a new line and make sure to add the original page numbers in the margin.

The **extent of your notes** depends on whether or not you will be able to consult the original books and articles when you come to write the first draft of the essay. If you have your own copy of each of the key references, it may be that the headings and paragraph themes you listed earlier are sufficient. If you are using library materials which are on short-term loan, you may have to write out an extensive set of notes. For example, you may come across a chapter which gives some detailed statistical information about mortality (death) and morbidity (illness) for different social groups in different countries. If you have to return the book to the library in the next day or so, you will need to decide immediately which information you will probably use in the essay and make a careful note of the figures, which groups they refer to, when they were collected, and so on. With access to the original work a very brief note would be sufficient to remind you that this is a valuable source of mortality and morbidity data. If you have only limited access to a paper or chapter that is obviously going to be a very useful source of information, photocopy the relevant sections if you can afford it. The time you spend on photocopying will be more than offset by the reduction in your essay preparation time — your author notes will be much briefer, and you can mark your photocopy to direct your attention immediately to the relevant passages rather than having to scan the full page of the unmarked library original.

It is likely that the **same point will be made by several authors**. For example, one of the first papers you read might point out that there is a long-standing association between certain jobs and certain diseases. You think it is important and add it to your author notes. Later, you find that the same point is made by two other authors. However, it is not necessary to note the same fact two or three times, and so the more you read the more selective you become with your note-making. With your first paper, all relevant comments are new and thus worth noting. By the time you read your fifth (or ninth, or twelfth) paper, you will largely ignore what that author says about issues that are now very familiar to you.

However, keep an eye open for particularly **interesting examples of old ideas**. For example, one author points out that the phrase 'mad as a hatter' is based on fact — workers in the hat industry were affected by mercury in the felting material used to make the hats. If you think that the general point about jobs and diseases is worth illustrating with this example, add it to your author notes. You should also make an additional note when you come across particularly **well-expressed accounts of old ideas** which you might use as direct quotations. For example, recall the quote that 'carelessness, gluttony, drunkenness, and sloth take some of their wages in illness' (Kass 1975, p. 31). In a very direct way this phrase captures much of the conservative explanation of varying rates of illness among social classes. It is therefore worth noting down in full for possible inclusion as a quote in your essay.

Section notes

You now need to move from a collection of author notes to a collection of section notes. To do this you have to **rearrange your notes to fit the main sections of your basic essay plan**. So far, you have identified in the literature those facts and ideas which are relevant to your essay topic. But the facts and ideas in your author notes are in the order used by the original authors. These notes now need to be reordered so that they appear under the section headings listed in your basic essay plan. Work down the list of headings making up the essay plan, writing each heading on the top of a separate A4 sheet. You should also have a 'Miscellaneous' sheet for any notes which, although obviously saying something about the essay topic, don't quite fit into any of the structure plan headings. If there turns out to be a lot of them you will need to reconsider the structure of your essay.

You then need to go through your author notes and **assign each comment to a particular section sheet**. For example, you would place a point about how the working class make relatively poor use of preventative health services on the 'conservative–consumption' sheet. The transfer of facts and ideas from author to section sheets can be done using scissors and paste. The method is suitable if you have been careful to always start each new point on a fresh line and to write on only one side of the sheet. You will have to make sure that you add the author's name and year of publication on the subject sheets. Alternatively, you can rewrite the author notes. An abbreviated version of the original notes will suffice — you can check back to either your earlier notes or the original text, providing you remember to always include the author's name, the year and the page number.

With the new section notes you are now able to do a more detailed plan of the essay. Under each heading you need to present the material in a structured, logical way. The basic sections on the outline plan are still too broad to allow you to start writing just yet. Instead, you need more **specific themes**. For example, I found that my notes on the radical health model of the production process had three general themes: (1) dangerous industrial substances; (2) the general organisation of the production process; and (3) the political environment in which the production process operates. These analytical subcategories provide a logical development of the argument, each dealing with progressively more general areas of concern. These three themes may or may not appear as formal subheadings in the final essay, but either way subheadings are needed in the detailed essay plan. Although not as difficult as drawing up the basic essay plan — you are now much more familiar with the material — identifying analytical subcategories from your section notes is not always plain sailing. You must be prepared to spend considerable time and effort over this important part of the essay development process. When I completed this second, more detailed round of planning for the social class and illness essay, I had the detailed essay plan shown in Figure 3.6.

You are now at the stage where **any further ordering of the material is best done as you begin to write your first draft** of the essay. Essay writing is too creative a process to imagine that you can plan it out to the last paragraph. When you come to organise your notes for a new theme (e.g. conservative views about dangerous industrial substances) you may well find that you have relatively little information. You therefore need to make a further search of the literature, but now your task is much more straightforward as you know exactly the sort of material you are looking for. You may be able to follow up additional sources using your lecturer's reading list, the bibliographies in your key references, your library's subject catalogue, or some of the indexing and abstracting journals considered in Chapter 2.

1. Introduction

2. Describing variations in illness between social classes

3. Explaining variations in illness between social classes
   • Class → Illness, and Illness → Class

   3.1 Radical arguments about the production process
      • dangerous industrial substances
      • general organisation of the production process
      • political environment in which production process operates

   3.2 Conservative counter-arguments about the production process
      • counter-arguments about dangerous industrial substances
      • counter-arguments about general organisation
      • counter-arguments about political environment

   3.3 Conservative arguments about the consumption process
      • diet
      • smoking
      • preventative health services

   3.4 Radical counter-arguments about the consumption process
      • counter-arguments about diet
      • counter-arguments about smoking
      • counter-arguments about preventative health services

4. Conclusion

Figure 3.6 Social class and illness: detailed essay plan

Writing an essay

It is important to emphasise that writing the essay is an ongoing process, not a once-only activity. Your words are not written in stone. You should expect to change them as you think of better ways to order your ideas and better words to express them. It follows then that the easier it is to change your text, the easier it is to produce an essay of high quality. This is where **word processing** comes into its own. The term itself indicates that writing is a process rather than a once-only activity. Once your text is typed onto a computer file, it is an easy matter to make both major and minor changes — from reordering the sequence of major sections to correcting a single punctuation mark. Most tertiary institutions now have computer equipment available for student use. If word processing is not part of your degree program, find out if there is an optional short course in word processing. The skills you learn from enrolling in such a course will be extremely useful to you throughout your entire student career (and probably beyond). If word processing equipment is not available, a second-hand typewriter can often be bought quite cheaply (my typewriter cost $30 in 1989). It can, of course, be shared. With practice you can type a paper as quickly as you can legibly write it in longhand.

Typeface, whether produced by a printer or a typewriter, has the advantage of distancing you from what you have written. In other words, when your ideas are recorded in an impersonal typeface rather than in your own unique handwriting, **you can look more objectively at what you have written**. The more objective you are about your work the more likely you are to see its faults, and the more likely you are to correct them.

The message then comes across loud and clear — **type it, don't write it**. Indeed, a handwritten final paper is becoming a rarity in some areas of Australian tertiary education, with some lecturers following the lead of many of their American counterparts and insisting on printed or typed papers for assessment.

The most efficient method is to write your **first draft of the essay** directly onto a computer file as it saves writing the text in longhand and then typing it. However, this can be difficult in a crowded, noisy computer room. Even if you have your own personal computer at home you may, like me, prefer to think with a pen or pencil in your hand. Thus, the first handwritten draft of this section of the chapter was a mass of deletions and additions as I made the first of many rounds of changes to the existing text. It was then typed onto a computer file and looked at very critically on several occasions to improve the structure and style. On each occasion I worked on a fresh copy of the section, produced by a printer linked to a personal computer. This meant that I could work on the current version without being distracted by the many earlier changes, as these disappeared each time I updated the file.

It's unlikely you will have quite as much time to spend on **essay revision**. However, at the *very least* you should plan to: (1) write the first draft in longhand, revising as you go; (2) reread the first draft and make further handwritten changes; (3) type the second draft onto a computer file, again revising as you go; (4)

print out the third draft and revise once again; and (5) print out the fourth and final version for submission. If you don't have access to a word processor you should type up the handwritten draft with wide margins and double-spacing to give you plenty of room to make changes. When you are satisfied that you have made all the improvements possible in the time available, you will then need to retype the entire paper.

The process of essay writing basically entails using your notes and the original texts to help you produce a paper which is logically structured, well-written and attractively laid out. I'll say more about each — structure, style and layout — in turn.

Essay structure

For the lecturer, reading an essay means entering into new territory. Going somewhere new is always easier if you have a map and if there are signposts to guide you. Without them there is a danger that you will end up being lost — which usually is not a very rewarding experience! The moral of the story, of course, is that your essay should contain the literary equivalents of a map and signposts.

Introduction

In an essay the equivalent of a map is the introduction. Its primary role is to **leave readers in no doubt that the essay has a clear and reasonable structure**. In other words, you should outline the major sections to be covered and briefly say why you have chosen this particular structure. This could include the reasons why you have limited the essay to a particular time or place, and why you have concentrated on a particular aspect of a much larger social phenomenon (e.g. cars to illustrate manufacturing industry, Christianity to illustrate religion, or cancer to illustrate illness). For example, the introduction to the social class and illness essay could read like this:

> In capitalist countries such as Australia and Britain, the overall level of illness is much higher in the working class than the middle class. However, there is no generally accepted explanation of this difference. Basically, radicals argue that working class individuals suffer more illness because of their generally

less healthy environment — in particular their working conditions in the capitalist production process. What is needed to improve health is a basic change in the way capitalist society is structured. In contrast, conservatives argue that the working class lifestyle in general, and consumption patterns in particular, are a major cause of illness. It is up to individuals to adopt a more healthy — more middle class — way of living. The paper reflects this debate between radical and conservative commentators.

The essay has the following structure. A short descriptive section reviews the statistical evidence about class and illness. It concentrates on British statistics, because these are the most comprehensive and up-to-date available for an advanced, capitalist society. The main body of the essay examines the radical and conservative explanations of the difference in illness rates between social classes, focusing first on the production process, and then on the consumption process. Because radicals concentrate primarily on production, and conservatives primarily on consumption, the essay first outlines the radicals' production arguments, followed by the conservatives' counter-

arguments; it then looks at the conservatives' consumption arguments, followed by the radicals' counter-arguments. These arguments and counter-arguments are clearly shown in the debate about the causes of cancer, and the essay focuses on this literature to illustrate more general points about illness and social class.

Headings

If the introduction provides a map for the essay, **the headings provide a series of signposts** along the way. There is a tradition in some schools to prohibit the use of headings in essays. I can't see why. All textbooks and virtually all journal articles include headings for the benefit of their readers. I strongly recommend that you provide headings in your essays, unless your lecturer specifically advises otherwise. Just one word of caution is necessary. Take care to prepare readers for the transition from one headed section to the next. This usually involves adding a linking sentence, either at the end of the preceding section or at the beginning of the new one. This can also serve to remind readers of the structure of the essay, and where they are at this particular point. For example, in the social class and illness essay (see Figure 3.6), the transition between the 'Radical–production' and 'Conservative–production' sections could read as follows: 'Having considered radical arguments about how the capitalist production process affects workers' health, I now turn to the major conservative counter-arguments'.

I suggest that in an essay of only a few thousand words you **use no more than two levels of heading** — more than this can get rather confusing. Distinguish between major and minor headings by using different typefaces. Generally, keep your layout as simple as possible. Using upper case (i.e. capitals) for major headings and lower case for minor headings is all that is needed if each heading is on a separate line. If you wish to give added emphasis, underline the heading or use a bold type. Numbering your headings as shown in Figure 3.6 also helps your readers to see exactly where they are in the development of the essay.

Paragraphs

If the headings are the signposts, then the paragraphs under them represent distance markers along the way. Paragraphs are, in ef-

fect, **short unheaded sections**. Like their longer, headed counterparts, each paragraph should be devoted to one theme. As I
mentioned earlier, quite often the first sentence sets the theme for
the rest of the paragraph — as in this paragraph. You will already
have identified the major themes, and added them to the detailed
essay plan (the items next to the bullets (•) in Figure 3.6). In a
short essay you might deal with each listed theme in a single
paragraph. In a longer essay, more paragraphs may be needed,
each developing a subtheme. For example, in the section on radical
arguments about the production process, the first theme is about
dangerous industrial substances. In a fairly long essay this could
be split into two paragraphs: the first could give examples of
the long-established and officially recognised link between certain
occupations and diseases; the second could show how occupational
diseases are much more common than official figures suggest.

When writing the first draft of a new paragraph it is useful to
start by jotting down its **basic theme**. This helps you to check and
see whether you're sticking to the point. A theme, or even subtheme,
cannot be adequately covered in a single sentence. Don't follow
the lead of the tabloid press and start each new sentence on a
new line. Because it starts on a new line, the new sentence is
seen by readers to indicate the start of a new theme. They soon
become tired and annoyed at being misled! At the other extreme
there is the 'paragraph' that takes up an entire section — starting
immediately under one heading and stopping immediately before
the next. In all but the shortest essay, most sections are broad
enough to cover two or more themes. A single paragraph containing more than one theme again leaves readers feeling tired and
annoyed as they have to do a job that the writer should do —
providing 'natural breaks' in the text by showing where one theme
ends and the next begins. Even worse are long paragraphs in
which two or more themes have been jumbled together, producing
a confused mixture of ideas that the poor reader has to try to
unscramble.

Generally, the **length of a paragraph** should be one-quarter
to three-quarters of a typed page with one-and-a-half-spacing or
double-spacing. Use shorter or longer paragraphs rarely and
be able to justify their use. For example, the basic message of
several preceding paragraphs may be summarised in a couple
of sentences and given a separate paragraph to emphasise its
importance, as I have done here. Or you can introduce the

basic message of several following paragraphs, as I do in the next paragraph.

Conclusion

You obviously want to leave your readers with a favourable impression of your essay. It makes sense that what they have read most recently they will remember most clearly. Consequently, what appears at the end — the conclusion — should be the *pièce de résistance* of the essay — the **jewel in the crown**! Like jewels, each conclusion has many facets, but generally in your conclusion you should do two things — look back and describe the most important points of your work and, where appropriate, look forward and prescribe future courses of action. I'll look at each in turn, starting with the descriptive role of the conclusion.

Description   Your conclusion has to leave your reader in no doubt about the main points raised in the paper. In virtually all tertiary-level essays these will include both **the facts and your interpretation of them**. If the essay title is framed as a direct question (e.g. 'To what extent . . .?', 'Is it true that . . .?', 'Do you agree that . . .?') it is important that your conclusion gives a direct answer. It need not necessarily be a clear-cut one — you might agree 'in part' or believe that it is true 'to some extent'. What is required is a reasoned answer based on the facts and ideas you have presented. Your answer should rarely come as a surprise to your readers who, with your help, have been assessing the material as they have read through the main body of the essay.

Similar comments apply to comparative essays, especially ones which compare explanations about why certain things occur. You often have to adopt the role of judge and jury, using the evidence to give a verdict. Often, however, the courtroom analogy breaks down. A result of 'Slightly guilty' or 'Generally innocent' may be appropriate if you find that the most strongly supported view consists of a combination of aspects of two or more sets of arguments. For example, in the social class and illness essay you may conclude that working conditions do play a significant role in generating higher rates of illness among members of the working class — but so also do their generally unhealthier lifestyles. However, *apportioning* blame (e.g. 60% working conditions, 40% lifestyle) may not be possible given the complexity of the question and the paucity of the available evidence.

Prescription As well as looking back and describing the main points of the essay, your conclusion may also look forward and **prescribe a course of action** for researchers, governments and others. For example, if the descriptive part shows that there is not enough evidence to make a judgement about an issue, you might pinpoint what you think are the most important areas in which researchers need to do more work. More generally, much of what you study in the social sciences forms part of the public policy agenda — unemployment, housing, crime, health care and a host of other issues. Occasionally you may feel that the evidence you have presented indicates the need for a particular course of action. If so, highlight this in the final part of your essay. The fact that you appreciate the potential application of your findings will almost certainly result in your getting a higher mark for the essay. It will also help you develop a way of thinking that could be very valuable later in your career.

As I have pointed out, the conclusion is the last and usually the most important part of the paper. **The importance of the conclusion should be reflected in the time you spend on it.** If done properly, what is often the shortest section can take the longest time to prepare. Unfortunately, the conclusion comes at the end of what may well be an arduous, even exhausting, writing experience. Consequently, the most important part of the essay can become the least important in terms of time spent on it. A few sentences are dashed off, pretty much repeating what has been said in the introduction — despite the obvious fact that an opening section has a very different purpose from that of a closing section.

You should **complete the rest of the essay before you begin the concluding section**. You can then read the introduction and main body of the essay with the minimum of distractions, concentrating on the overall impression given by the essay. When you write the conclusion you will be able to ensure that it is in step with the rest of the paper, and you will be in a better position to see the wider implications raised by the paper. One possible conclusion to the class and illness essay is as follows:

> The literature reviewed in this essay shows that in advanced capitalist societies, members of the working class suffer more illness than do members of the middle class. The view that such differences are undesirable is one that has unanimous support. Upgrading the health status of the most disadvan-

taged is the universally accepted strategy for eradicating such inequalities. But at this point the consensus ends, for disagreement over the causes of the problem leads to disagreement over methods for its solution.

Thus, the radicals' emphasis on work-related issues leads them to the view that the higher level of illness among the working class is because the capitalist system is inherently harmful to the health of its workers, especially those in low status jobs. The radicals' solution is to reconstruct the capitalist system. In contrast, the conservatists' emphasis on home-related issues leads them to the view that the higher level of illness among the working class is because of their misuse of the freedoms and prosperity that the capitalist system provides. The conservatives' solution is for the working class to change their consumption patterns so that they resemble those of the healthier middle class.

From the evidence presented in this paper, it is not possible to make a judgement on the relative explanatory power of each school of thought. However, although their main areas of emphasis are very different, the conservative and radical health models do still have considerable areas of overlap. For example, most conservatives acknowledge the health damaging effects of certain industrial chemicals, and most radicals acknowledge that smoking is the most important single cause of cancer.

These overlaps are important when looking at how to reduce health inequalities. Proposals obviously need to be attuned to existing political realities, and currently the trend is for governments to become less involved in the workings of the market place. Consequently, the major agent of change in the production process will have to be the trade unions. They will have to make their members and the general public more conscious of industrial health hazards, and they will have to give greater priority to health and safety issues in their negotiations with employers. However, with regard to the consumption process, even a government committed to a policy of minimum market intervention must surely support the idea that people should make an *informed* choice when they adopt a particular lifestyle. This implies that there needs to be a greater political commitment to health education programs, particularly those concerning smoking.

Essay style

I now turn from essay structure to essay style. In effect, I am shifting my attention from sections and paragraphs to sentences and words. Your aim is to develop a writing style which will communicate your ideas as clearly and concisely as possible. To do this you must have a working knowledge of both the general conventions about writing in English and the more specialist, academic conventions about writing in the social sciences and humanities. I'll look at each in turn.

General writing conventions

To write well you must have a suitably large vocabulary of English words and a working knowledge about the rules for linking words together. Much of the class time of primary and secondary students is spent learning these skills. Consequently, most tertiary students should be proficient in writing English. There are exceptions, of course. Your first language may not be English, or you may have returned to formal study after many years with little or

no recent writing experience. If so, you may need extra help with spelling and grammar. An increasing number of tertiary institutions are running refresher courses on basic writing skills. If necessary, check to see if your college or university has such a course. Alternatively, there are numerous English grammar books. One of the best is *A Survival Kit for Writing English* (Bailey 1984). I make use of some the ideas from this excellent book in the following paragraphs.

It isn't appropriate here to provide a crash course in the fundamentals of using the English language. However, it is useful to highlight some of the major difficulties I've noticed when marking student assignments. I'll start with individual words, and then move onto the rules about grammar and punctuation that are used when linking words together.

Selecting and spelling words With regard to individual words, the first step is to select the right one and the second step is to spell it correctly. Usually, the incredibly powerful portable computer inside your head has no difficulty in **selecting the right word**. Sometimes, however, it does need some help. If you're unsure about the exact meaning of a word, then obviously you need to check it in your dictionary. In theory this should prevent you from misusing any word. However, there are many common words which are often misused because they sound the same as, or similar to, other words which have different meanings (e.g. to, too, two). Because of the simplicity of each word on its own, writers can easily misuse it — it looks just too straightforward to bother checking in a dictionary.

Two **pairs of words which still frequently cause problems** at tertiary level are *there* (as in *here and there*) and *their* (meaning *belonging to them*), and *its* (meaning *belonging to it*) and *it's* (short for *it is*). Less common, but just as troublesome, are: affect/effect, breach/breech, complement/compliment, dependent/dependant, and so on through the rest of the alphabet. There are specialised publications to help you, such as *The Penguin Dictionary of Troublesome Words* (Bryson 1987). Shorter lists appear in more general texts such as *A Pocket Guide to Written English* (Temple 1978).

There are also occasions when you have an idea but can't think of an appropriate word to express it. In this situation a **thesaurus** is usually more useful than a dictionary. A thesaurus is simply a list of words categorised by topic. The words under each topic are, in turn, subdivided according to whether they are nouns, adjectives, verbs or adverbs. For example, in my well-worn *Roget's Thesaurus* (1966) under the heading 'List' comes nouns such as enumeration, file, electoral roll, and thesaurus. Also listed are verbs such as index, itemise, and register. If, for example, I couldn't recall the name for the list of voters in an area, I could use the index in the thesaurus to find the heading 'List', and then look through the list of nouns to find the term I need. (Alternatively, I could find the term by looking under 'Voter' in the index.) You can buy a paperback edition of a thesaurus for only a few dollars. As it is potentially useful in every piece of writing you do, it is certainly money well spent. Some word processing packages include a thesaurus. If you have access to one make sure you find out how to use it.

I'll now move on from selecting words to **spelling** them. The best way to improve your spelling is to read widely. You become familiar with seeing a word spelled a certain way and, usually without thinking, you adopt this same spelling in your own work. Of course, it's not a foolproof method. There are some words that, no matter how often I see them, I always have to check (e.g. occurred, offered), and there are others that I come across so rarely that I need to recheck them each time (e.g. defendant, caricature).

There are some **spelling rules**, the most useful probably being: *I before e except after c, or when sounded as 'a', as in neighbour and weigh*. So, for example, it is 'chief' and 'achieve' with *ie* following the *h*, but it is 'perceive' and 'receive' with *ei* following the *c*, and 'freight' and 'rein' with the *ei* pronounced as *a*. Many spelling rules are quite complicated, and even if you can remember the rule there is no guarantee that your specific word isn't one of the exceptions (e.g. 'seize' and 'ancient' are two exceptions to the above rule). The best advice about spelling is: **if in doubt, check it out**.

I've included an appendix to the book which will be useful. The ***1000 commonly misspelled words*** is a list that I've drawn up over several years. Each time I see a new spelling error in a student essay, or each time I have to consult the dictionary to check a word myself, I add it to the list. I suggest that you add other words that you have difficulty spelling, especially those on returned essays that have been corrected by your lecturer. Adding them to the list will help you to remember the spelling. Photocopy the list, and put it in the front of your working file. You will be surprised at just how useful it will be. Of course, it doesn't do away with the need for a dictionary — you still need to check the spelling before adding a word to the list.

If you're using a word processing package it's likely that it will include a **spell-checker**. This is an electronic dictionary that checks each word you type in against its own list of words and indicates which of your words do not appear on its list. It is also useful for picking up typing errors (e.g. 'becuase' instead of 'because'). Again, you will need your own dictionary to check words highlighted by the spell-checker that you are unsure about. It may be that you have spelled a word incorrectly, or it could be that you have got it right but the word isn't in the electronic dictionary, or it could be that your Australian spelling is different from the dictionary's American spelling (e.g. 'travelled' (Australian) and 'traveled' (American)). Remember, however, that a spell-checker does not show where words have been spelled correctly but used incorrectly.

There are two final points about individual words. The first relates to the use of **apostrophes**. An apostrophe is used with a noun to show possession (e.g. the cat's mat — i.e. the mat belonging to the cat). If the noun is plural and ends in *s*, usually the apostrophe is added without a second *s* (e.g. the cats' mats — i.e. the mats belonging to the cats). Don't use an apostrophe with a plural noun when possession is not intended (e.g. The cats sat on the mat). Note that an apostrophe is not used in yours, hers (or his!), ours, theirs or its (e.g. The cat sat on its mat). In this example, *its* indicates possession — the mat belongs to the cat. As well as showing possession, an apostrophe can also show that two words have been contracted into one by leaving out some letters (e.g. I've seen the cat — it's sitting on its mat). In this example, *I've* is short for *I have* and *it's* is short for *it is*.

Finally, I'll make a few comments about **capital letters**. Generally, limit your use of capital initial letters to the beginning of each sentence, the pronoun *I*, and the names of specific people, places or things (e.g. The cat I own sat on the Persian mat). Sometimes the same word can be used in both a specific and general sense (e.g. Deakin University is one of several universities in Victoria). A capital letter is appropriate when referring to Deakin University in particular, but a small letter is used when referring to Victorian universities in general.

Grammar Before you can link individual words into meaningful groups you need to have a working knowledge of the rules of English grammar. Individual words are grouped together into what Bailey (1984, Chapter 2) terms 'control units' and 'support units' which, in turn, may be grouped together to form sentences. Each sentence must include at least one control unit (more traditionally known as a main clause). A control unit is made up of two groups of words: a subject group and a verb group. For example, in 'The cat sat on the mat', the phrase 'The cat' forms the subject group and 'sat on the mat' forms the verb group. Together, therefore, the two groups of words form a control unit. A control unit on its own forms the simplest sentence.

A verb group on its own does not form a sentence. Some verb-forms are incomplete in that they cannot be attached directly to a subject and therefore cannot be used as the main verb in a sentence. The **present participle** is the verb-form that causes most problems (e.g. The cat sitting on the mat). In this example, the present participle (sitting) needs changing to a verb-form which can be attached directly to a subject (e.g. The cat sat on the mat).

The distinction between complete and incomplete verbs seems pretty obvious from this example, but similar errors often occur in student essays (e.g. The radical interpretation being the one most supported by the evidence). Here the student has incorrectly used the word 'being', the present participle of the verb 'to be', as the main verb. Instead, the sentence needs a simple 'is' (i.e. The radical interpretation is . . .).

The present participle of a verb also appears in the problem of **danglers**. These are phrases which are left dangling. In other words, they are phrases which are not connected with what they are meant to describe (e.g. Sitting on top of the flagpole, I watched the cat). In this example, 'Sitting on top of the flagpole' is dangling: it has become separated from what it is designed to describe — 'the cat'. All that is needed is a repositioning of the dangling phrase (e.g. I watched the cat sitting on top of the flagpole). Not surprisingly, the past participle of a verb also causes dangling problems (e.g. Sat on top of the flagpole, I . . .).

Finally in this list of common grammatical faults, I'll look at the need to use the **right case for pronouns**. Most pronouns vary depending on whether they are the subject of the sentence and thus part of the subject group (I, he, she, we, they), or whether they are the object of the sentence and thus part of the verb group (me, him, her, us, them). Thus, it is 'I saw him' (I = subject, him = object) but 'He saw me' (He = subject, me = object). The fact that there is more than one subject or more than one object docs not change this word use (e.g. Tom and I saw him. He saw Tom and me). In the first example, 'Tom and I' make up the subject of the sentence. In the second example, 'Tom and me' form the object of the sentence. If in doubt, read out the sentence with just the pronoun as the subject (. . . I saw him) or object (He saw . . . me).

Two of the most troublesome pronouns are **who** and **whom**. Traditionally, the practice has been to use 'who' to refer to the subject of a sentence (e.g. The man who saw me . . .), and 'whom' to refer to the object (e.g. The man whom I saw . . .). Although in theory the rule is a simple one, in practice it has long confused writers including Shakespeare, Dickens, Somerset Maugham and me. (Rarely am I in such exalted company!) Fortunately, the pragmatists are slowly overcoming the grammarians and it is becoming increasingly acceptable to use 'who' as both subject and object, except for well-known phrases such as 'To whom it may concern', and 'For whom the bell tolls'.

Punctuation Having looked briefly at spelling and grammar problems, I'll now talk about punctuation. Bailey (1984, p. 3) stresses
the general importance of punctuation, pointing out that 'Spoken
meaning depends on intonation; written meaning depends on
punctuation'. Basically, **punctuation helps make clear the
meaning of the text** by separating the control and support units.
There are two major groups of punctuation marks: middle stops,
or marks that go inside a sentence (the comma, semicolon, colon,
dash and brackets); and end stops, or marks that go at the end of
a sentence (the full stop, exclamation mark and question mark).
The most commonly occurring problems relate to the use of middle
stops, particularly commas, semicolons and colons. I'll concentrate
on these in the following paragraphs.

Generally, **middle stops go *between* units** rather than within
units. For example, 'The cat sat on the mat' is a control unit which
forms a simple sentence. It does not need any punctuation within
it. The rule is simple enough, yet one of the most common punctuation errors is to separate the subject group and the verb group
with a **comma** (e.g. The cat, sat on the mat). In contrast, a
support unit does need separating from its control unit by a comma
(e.g. Sitting on the mat, the cat watched the bird). Here 'Sitting on
the mat' is the support unit and 'the cat watched the bird' is the
control unit. The separating comma helps to make clear the meaning of the sentence.

You use commas *inside* a control unit or support unit only in
two circumstances. The first is when you have a list of two or
more adjectives describing the same noun (e.g. The big, black cat
sat on the mat). The second circumstance is when you have a
support unit positioned inside a control unit (e.g. The cat, sitting
on the mat, watched the bird). In this example, 'sitting on the mat'
is a support unit inside a control unit (The cat . . . watched the
bird) and is separated from it by a pair of commas. A fairly
common error is to use a pair of commas to form a control and
support unit from a group of words which correctly form a single
control unit. Consider the following example: 'Cats, which are
black, bring good luck'. Here the punctuation divides a control
unit (Cats . . . bring good luck) from a support unit (which are
black). But, of course, it is only black cats that are supposed to
bring good luck. Not all cats are black — though the sentence
suggests this. In fact, the sentence is formed from the single
control unit made up of a subject group (Cats which are black)

and a verb group (bring good luck). The commas are definitely not needed.

So far I have concentrated on the use of commas. The comma is the most commonly used middle stop; it is also the weakest. A less commonly used middle stop is the **semicolon** (;). It's a punctuation middleweight, lying midway between the comma and the full stop. (Notice that it's made up of both a comma and a full stop.) Not surprisingly, therefore, it's used in those situations when a comma is too light and a full stop too heavy. It's most commonly used when you have two closely related control units. Although it may be technically possible to divide them with a full stop, in terms of writing style it's a rather heavy-handed form of punctuation (e.g. It was a good cat. It never brought in rats). On the other hand, by itself a comma is too lightweight for the job (e.g. It was a good cat, it never brought in rats). This is an occasion when a semicolon — not too heavy, not too light — comes in handy (e.g. It was a good cat; it never brought in rats). I'll come back to semicolons in the following discussion of colons.

The basic function of the **colon** is to introduce text that explains, expands, or summarises the preceding text. For example, the colon is often used to introduce a quotation: 'It brings the sentence to a sudden, temporary halt and gives a cue for the quotation which is waiting in the wings' (Bailey 1984, p. 62). However, be careful not to use the colon (or any other punctuation mark for that matter) in a mechanical fashion. Make sure that your quote is sufficiently important to warrant bringing the sentence 'to a sudden, temporary halt'. If it isn't, then 'Something gentler is needed' (Bailey 1984, p. 63). As the previous sentence shows, a less disruptive comma may be adequate.

Another common role for the colon is to introduce a list of items. Recall how I said earlier that there were two basic types of punctuation mark: middle stops, or marks used in the middle of a sentence; and end stops, or marks used at the end of a sentence. In the previous sentence, the colon introduces the list. Notice that the two main items in the list — middle stops and end stops — are separated by a semicolon. This is because the weaker comma is used to separate the name from the definition inside each item in the list (e.g. 'middle stops, or marks used . . .'). There are thus three levels of punctuation in the sentence: the colon, used to separate the introduction from the list; the semicolon, used to separate items in the list; and the commas, used to separate the parts of each item. The full stop marks the end of the list.

Finally in this review of punctuation problems, I'll briefly mention the remaining middle stops and end stops: **dashes, brackets, question marks and exclamation marks**. The simplest advice is to avoid using them. Exclamation marks and dashes are both rather flamboyant and more suited to writing less formal than an academic essay — don't you think! What about question marks? In an undergraduate paper the main job is to answer questions, not to ask them. Textbook writers often begin a section by asking a question, and spend the rest of the section answering it. But your essays are not part of a textbook, and rhetorical questions such as the one above are not needed. Round brackets enclose 'asides' or additional information. You usually find that your essay draft has exceeded the word limit and you have to cut out material. It doesn't make sense to leave in those parts which, by their position inside brackets, are obviously additional to the main text.

In my comments on spelling problems I urged you to use a computer-based spell-checker. Less common, but still useful, are computer-based **grammar checkers**, such as *Correct Grammar*, *Grammatik*, and *MacProof*. These packages will help you identify most of the spelling, grammar and punctuation problems outlined above — plus a lot more. In addition to identifying problems, these packages also explain them and suggest possible solutions. If you have access to this sort of software I would advise you to use it.

Academic writing conventions

In addition to the general conventions relating to writing in English, there are the more specific conventions relating to academic writing in the social sciences and humanities. I'll discuss three of these: language bias, tone or level of formality, and acknowledging and referencing sources.

Language bias Language bias is the way in which language reflects and helps maintain the social status quo (Betts and Seitz 1986, p. 76). Social groups have different degrees of influence on the way society is run. For example, at the broadest level men are more powerful than women, and the middle class is more powerful than the working class. Similarly, the structure of the English language has developed to project a male, middle-class world. In other words, there is gender bias and class bias in language.

I'll look firstly at the issue of **gender bias**. How does language reflect and help maintain women's subordinate social position? Most importantly, language makes women 'invisible' by allowing masculine nouns and pronouns to refer to both men and women. Consider the following two examples: (1) 'Man shares the planet with many other animals'; and (2) 'If any reader wants to comment on this book, he should write to me'. In the first example, all women are implicitly included in the noun 'Man', and in the second example, each female reader is included in the pronoun 'he'. Even when women are specifically mentioned they are often stereotyped, trivialised and shown to be dependent on men. For example, why is it that in news reports the physical appearance and marital status of women seem to be so much more important than that of men?

Non-sexist writing is now the convention in the social sciences, and is being taken more seriously in other areas — as shown, for example, by the inclusion of a chapter on non-sexist language in the most recent edition of the Australian government's *Style Manual for Authors, Editors and Printers* (1988, Chapter 8). The chapter provides a wealth of practical advice on how to avoid gender bias in your writing. I'll concentrate on the problem that you will face most frequently when writing essays — how to **avoid using 'he' and 'his' to refer to both sexes**. Recall an earlier example: 'If any reader wants to comment on this book, he should write to me'. How can this sentence be rewritten in a non-sexist way? The problem is that the English language doesn't have a gender-neutral, third-person singular pronoun that can be applied to people. Of the three possible pronouns — he, she, it — 'it' is the obvious choice, but this word is used almost exclusively to refer to things, not people. Occasionally you see 'it' used to refer to a baby (e.g. The baby has dropped its rattle). Less frequently, 'it' is used to refer to a child (e.g. The child knows its alphabet). But 'it' is never used to refer to an adult. (Perhaps this reflects the view that babies and children are not really people!)

Given the lack of a suitable singular pronoun, the simplest way of avoiding non-sexist language is to include a reference to both sexes: 'If any reader wants to comment on this book, he or she should write to me'. The term 'he or she' (or 'she or he') is preferable to 'he/she' or 's/he' because it can be deciphered immediately by the reader. However, although the phrases 'he and she' and 'his and her' are acceptable when used occasionally, they can become rather tiresome to read if your essay is peppered with them. Another possibility is to make the subject of the sentence plural and use the gender-neutral pronoun 'they': 'If readers have comments about this book, they should write to me'. A third method is to **eliminate the third person pronoun**: 'Any reader wanting to comment on this book should write to me' or, more simply, 'Any reader with comments about this book should write to me'. Eliminating the pronoun is usually the most satisfactory solution. (Incidentally, I *would* be interested in comments about the book. The address is DUW, PO Box 423, Warrnambool 3280.)

I'll briefly mention how to overcome other **less common difficulties regarding non-sexist writing**. There are always satisfactory alternatives to using 'man' to refer to both men and women: use people, humanity or the human race instead of man or mankind; use business executive or business manager for businessman; sales assistant or shop assistant for salesman; and even access hole or utility hole for manhole. Similarly, the *Style Manual* (1988, pp. 122–3) recommends that occupational terms that exclude men should be replaced by more general terms (e.g. cleaner for cleaning lady, and homemaker for housewife). Words such as authoress or actress which refer specifically to women and which are created by adding a feminine ending to a masculine word (author/ess) suggest that women are deviations from the masculine norm. Use the general term (author, actor) for everybody. Similarly, show women as participating equally with men by using generic terms such as doctor, lawyer and reporter for both women and men — avoid terms such as 'lady doctor' or 'female reporter'. Finally, bear in mind that the 'man' syllable in words such as 'manual' refers back to the Latin word *manus*, meaning hand — hence manual labour means hand labour. Thus, there is nothing odd grammatically in describing women as doing manual labour.

Secondly, how does language reflect **class bias** — in other words, how does it help maintain the subordinate social position of the working class? The argument here is that complex grammatical structures and difficult spelling conventions are linguistic barriers which help separate the working class from the middle class. As Betts and Seitz (1986, p. 76) point out, ' "Correct grammar" (like "correct accents") comes easily to people who already have advantages, and harder to those who do not'. Using this reasoning, it is not surprising that Prince Charles has come out strongly in defence of 'proper' standards of English grammar and spelling, or that standard English is referred to as 'the Queen's English'. Nor is it surprising that the less class-conscious Americans have spelling conventions that are simpler than those of the more class-conscious British (e.g. plow and plough). (Perhaps the defence of class privileges is one reason why the adoption of American spelling is so bitterly opposed by some people in Britain and Australia?)

However, this argument about class bias is not reflected in a liberal attitude about grammar and spelling in academic writing. Indeed, I have just spent some considerable time advising you to use standard English in your essays. Your image as a capable student suffers if your writing contains a large number of what are generally regarded as language errors. The reader's impression is that if you can't get right small technical details, it's more than likely that the rest of your work is badly flawed. This, of course, means that getting a degree is generally easier for Australian students from a middle-class, English-speaking background — which is one example of how language serves to maintain the status quo.

If you feel strongly that standard English is class-biased, you will be unhappy with the apparent double standards of the social sciences — being in the vanguard of eliminating gender bias but firmly supporting class bias. All I can suggest is that while you are a student you grit your teeth and follow the conventions. Later, if you wish, you can be a breaker of old conventions and a maker of new ones.

Tone The discussion of conventions in academic writing now turns to the issue of tone, or the **degree of formality required in an academic essay**. For example, the first piece of written work I ask from students on a social science skills course is a short account of the procedures and results of a library exercise. Some students pitch their accounts far too low (e.g. 'I was pretty sure that I'd draw a blank. Imagine my surprise when I found a great stack of books!'). Many more students pitch their accounts far too high (e.g. they don't go to read books, they 'proceed to peruse monographs'). I have deliberately exaggerated the two examples, but similar, if somewhat less crude, examples of the wrong choice of writing tone often occur in student essays.

A very informal style occurs relatively infrequently in student essays. When identified, it can usually be corrected fairly easily once the student realises that such a style should be confined to diaries and personal letters. A **very formal style** occurs much more frequently and is more difficult to correct. This is because students often see a similar style in published work. For example, as far back as the 1940s, social scientists were caricatured as never failing to use two long words when one short one would do, and as generally stating 'the obvious in terms of the unintelligible' (Williamson 1947, p. 17). Nearly thirty years later Harris and Blake (1976, p. 97) noted 'an excessive use of area jargon, complex sentence structures, and other smoke screens'. In the 1980s, the editors of one leading social science journal were so concerned about the same problem that they published a series of articles to help improve the writing skills of some of their colleagues (Selvin & Wilson 1984a, 1984b).

Keep your words and sentences as **simple** as possible. This doesn't mean, of course, that you should try to write the academic equivalent of an Enid Blyton story! Aim to produce an essay that will be understood immediately by a fellow student in your course. Don't deliberately avoid jargon or technical words as, once defined, they can provide a useful shorthand. Ideally, get a friend to listen as you read your draft essay out loud and ask them to give you some honest feedback. Admittedly, friends can be scarce on the ground at times like these! It will be easier if you offer to repay the favour. If you do, you will find that commenting on other people's writing also helps you to improve your own. If your friends always seem to be busy washing their hair or cleaning out the budgie's cage, you can always tape your reading and listen to the recording. However, it does take more time, and of course you don't get the benefit of someone else's critical comments. A third possibility is simply to listen to yourself reading the essay aloud. This is the least satisfactory method as it takes practice to concentrate simultaneously on reading and listening.

In the previous paragraph I suggested that you might co-operate with fellow students to improve your writing style. Of course, such co-operation could be extended to cover the entire essay writing process, providing that at the end of the day the essay you hand in is basically your own work, and that any help from other people is duly acknowledged. Certainly this is the academic convention when preparing articles and books for publication. If some of you are interested in forming a **mutual support writing group**, you should raise the idea with each of your course lecturers. Some lecturers may not be too enthusiastic, especially when all students in the group are working on the same essay. It is possible for a mutual support group to degenerate into one where lazy members end up taking much more than they contribute. However, this is unlikely to happen if the help of each group member is *individually* acknowledged in each essay, and if the group continues to make a forthright assessment of each member's contribution!

Having made a slight detour to discuss writing groups, I'll now return to the issue of writing style. Traditionally, social scientists have adopted the completely impersonal style used by physical scientists. Today, acceptable style in most of the social sciences is much less formal. The general preference now is for **direct sentence constructions**. Use the active voice of a verb (e.g. The cow jumped over the moon) rather than the passive voice (e.g. The moon was jumped over by the cow). For example, instead of the phrase 'It has been shown' use the more direct 'The paper shows'. Indeed, you might use the even more direct 'I show'. It seems to me that the phrase 'I show' is a marked improvement on the pompous-sounding 'The author shows' or 'The writer shows'. However, lecturers do differ in their views about this. Find out what each of your lecturers regards as an acceptable level of formality.

Not only is the active voice more informal, it can also be more informative. **The active voice reveals who is doing what** — the passive voice can conceal it. This brings to mind a story told by Paul Fussell (1989, pp. 296–7) about the D-day Allied landings in France during the Second World War. Just in case the plan proved unsuccessful, the soldier in charge, General Eisenhower, drafted a press statement saying that the landings had failed and that the troops had been withdrawn. On reflection he changed the wording to 'I have withdrawn the troops', so people could see where responsibility for the decision lay. In your essays, follow Eisenhower's lead and use the active rather than the passive voice.

Finally in this discussion of the level of formality in academic writing, I should point out that it is still generally **unacceptable to use contractions** such as *I'd, I've, isn't* or *didn't*. Contractions like these are confined to informally written textbooks — like this one. For once, then, the message is 'Do as I say, not as I do'.

Acknowledging and referencing sources Also related to academic writing style are the conventions about acknowledging and referencing your sources of information. No student essay at tertiary level is written without using other people's facts or ideas. Indeed, a basic characteristic of any science is that it builds on existing knowledge. You are not expected to reinvent the wheel each time you write an essay (though occasionally you might make it a little less squeaky). Just as you are expected to draw on other people's work, so too are you expected to acknowledge their help by saying exactly which parts of your essay have been taken from someone else's book or article. You are also expected to give sufficient information about each book or article to allow your reader to find it and follow up any point from it that you make in your work.

You are likely to come across **two basic systems of acknowledging and referencing sources**: (1) the Harvard or author/date system; and (2) the note system, which uses either footnotes positioned at the foot of each page or endnotes positioned together at the end of the chapter or article. The Harvard

system is the one used in this book. Sources of facts and ideas are acknowledged by adding the author's name, the year of publication and the page number next to the quotation in the body of the essay. In addition there is an alphabetical reference list at the end of the essay which gives all the details necessary for readers to follow up any book or article referred to in the essay. The note system uses numbers or special symbols (*, †, ‡, etc.) next to each quotation. These refer the reader to footnotes or endnotes, each of which provides details about the source of the quote and any other related matters the author thinks useful but not appropriate for the main text. An alphabetical list of all references at the end of the essay is optional in the note system.

Both systems have their **advantages and disadvantages**. For example, the need to include the author's name, the year of publication and the page number in the main text means that a Harvard citation can break up the flow of the text much more than the single number or symbol used in the note system. On the other hand, it is often much easier for the writer to type an essay using the Harvard system than the note system. Many word processing packages cannot handle footnoting, and even when you type (or write) the essay, it is often difficult to judge exactly how many footnotes you can include on a page. There are not the same page layout problems with the endnote system, but adding or deleting an endnote can result in the writer spending a good deal of time renumbering all the following endnotes. Which referencing system you use will depend largely on the type of degree you're enrolled in. For example, in sociology the Harvard system is generally used, while in history the note system is more widespread. I'll look at both, starting with the Harvard system.

Unfortunately, there is no general agreement about the exact format of the **Harvard system**. Generally, if you're given precise instructions by a course lecturer, follow them. For example, psychology staff generally use the format shown in the *Publication Manual of the American Psychological Association* (1983). If no advice is given, use the format outlined below which is taken from the Australian government's *Style Manual* (1988).

Firstly, I'll discuss how to acknowledge your sources within the body of the essay. These are known as **textual references** or **citations**. Quotations which are longer than about 30 or 40 words are identified as someone else's words by being indented (i.e. having a shorter line length than the rest of the text). Quotation marks aren't needed. The source is usually given at the end of the quote. For example:

> Quote materials exactly. Anything placed within quotation marks [or in an indented quote] should be the exact words found in the source. Do not alter verb tense, subject-verb agreement, or anything else about the quotation to make it fit into your text. Instead, change your text to conform to the quotation.
>
> Similarly, retain the original punctuation and emphasis when quoting materials . . .
>
> Sometimes quoted material contains mistakes of one kind or another: an awkward phrase or construction or a factual error . . . In such cases, attribute the odd phrase or expression to the source by placing the word "*sic*" after it in parentheses [i.e. round brackets]. This way your reader won't think your paper contains a misprint or typographical error . . .
>
> Finally, if you must alter the original quotation to include it properly in the text, identify any words you *add* by placing them in brackets [i.e. square brackets], not parentheses, inside of the quotation marks; indicate *omission* of any words by ellipses (three periods) (Cuba 1987, p. 122).

Notice that within the indented quote I follow Cuba's advice and use an ellipsis (. . .) each time I leave out parts of the original text (each is an example used by Cuba to illustrate a general point). If you shorten a quote, take care that you don't alter its meaning. If you add text (e.g. to define a term) place it inside square brackets as shown. Of course, a quotation full of omissions and deletions suggests that a quote is not really appropriate.

Similar rules apply to **quotes which are short enough for you to work into the structure of your text**. You identify each as a quote by the use of quotation marks, and give in brackets the author's surname, the year of publication and the page number. The exact format of the referencing can vary depending on whether or not the author's name is mentioned in the text. When it is not mentioned, 'it should be included in the citation, along with the date of publication, and sometimes the page number' (Cuba 1987, p. 124). On the other hand, as Cuba points out, when the author's name occurs in the text it 'is not repeated in the citation' (1987, p. 124).

In your citations, therefore, you need to give the **author**, the year of publication and the page number. If there are two or three individual authors, give the surnames of both or all of them (e.g. Bate & Sharpe 1990). If there are more than three authors, give the name listed first in the original text followed by 'et al.', an abbreviation of the Latin words *et alia*, meaning 'and others' (e.g. Guy et al. 1987). Occasionally no author's name is given. In this case, refer to the book or article by its title (e.g. *Subject Guide to Books in Print 1989–90*). To make the citations as unobtrusive as possible, a lengthy name is usually abbreviated after its first full listing (e.g. after my initial reference to the *Style Manual for Authors, Editors and Printers*, I refer simply to the *Style Manual*). Official reports can often cause problems. Occasionally, a specific person is shown as writing the report and he or she should be cited as the author. Usually, however, no specific author is acknowledged and you should cite the report under the name of the committee or department shown on the report. Once again, following the initial reference, you abbreviate a lengthy name to make the citations as unobtrusive as possible (e.g. 'According to a recent report from the Australian Bureau of Statistics (ABS 1991) . . .'). Finally, recall from Chapter 2 that there is an ongoing series called 'Parliamentary Papers' which include reports from Commonwealth government departments, commissions of inquiry and various parliamentary committees. You should cite parliamentary papers under the heading 'Australia, Parliament'. For example, in Chapter 2 the *Australian Bureau of Statistics: Annual Report 1988–89* is cited as 'Australia, Parliament 1989' because it is a parliamentary paper.

You can usually find the **year of publication** at the front of a book. Immediately after the title page is the imprint page which lists publishing details, including the date of publication. Often there will be only one year given. For example, the publishing notes in my copy of the Betts and Seitz book simply say 'First published in Australia 1986'. The citation for this book is, therefore, 'Betts and Seitz 1986'. Sometimes it is not quite this straightforward and two or more years may be listed. If so, always remember that the year you are interested in is the latest *publication* date. Additional copies of the same book may have been *reprinted* since then, but because nothing in the book has been changed it is the original publication date that you give. For example, the imprint page of my copy of a book by Harris and Blake says 'Copyright © 1976 . . . Reprinted 1981'. The citation for this book is therefore, 'Harris and Blake 1976'. Recall from Chapter 2 that a book can have more than one edition — that is, the author can revise and update an existing book. It continues to be sold under the original title but is designated as a new edition to show that it is substantially different from the earlier version. For example, my copy of *How to Write a Research Paper* by Ralph Berry gives the following publishing information: 'First edition 1966 Reprinted 1969, 1978 Second Edition 1986'. The latest publication date listed is 1986, and therefore the citation for this book is 'Berry 1986'.

Very occasionally, you may cite two sources written by the same author or authors in the same year. To avoid confusion use 'a' and 'b' to distinguish them. You may have noticed that I use this convention in the discussion of tone or formality to show that Selvin and Wilson had written two articles in the same year aimed at improving the writing skills of professional sociologists (Selvin & Wilson 1984a, 1984b).

When is it useful to include **direct quotes**, particularly long, indented quotes? Firstly, use direct quotes when the exact language helps to present the ideas in a memorable and sometimes colourful way. For example, recall the short quote that 'carelessness, gluttony, drunkenness, and sloth take some of their wages in illness' (Kass 1975, p. 31). This is such a memorable illustration of the conservative view of the association between illness and lifestyle that it deserves to be quoted directly. Similarly, the following longer quote illustrates very effectively the radical view of the basic conflict between workers' health and company profits in a capitalist system of production:

> Machines, buildings and arrangements of work are still designed to the cheapest specifications that will produce the goods at the greatest profit. Engineering design concentrates on the product and excludes the operator until the least possible moment. Safety, health and, last of all, comfort, are treated as bolt-on goodies (Kinnersly 1974, p. 195).

Secondly, quotes may be needed when introducing an idea around which much of the subsequent essay will revolve. Take, for example, concepts such as Robert Ardrey's 'territorial imperative', Charles H. Cooley's 'looking-glass self', or Ivan Illich's 'medical iatrogenesis'. Each concept needs careful definition, ideally using the originator's own words, before you can begin any evaluation.

So far I have discussed direct quotes, but often **you may use other authors' facts or ideas without using their exact words**. For example, recall that at the start of the language bias section I summarise an idea from a book by Betts and Seitz (1986, p. 76) by saying that language helps maintain the social status quo. Although I don't use their exact words, I do use their idea, and I am thus obliged to acknowledge them as my source. Including the page number in the reference is optional when you summarise or paraphrase, but it seems to me that the page number should be included as it might be useful to the reader.

There is no clear-cut dividing line between a summary or paraphrase of another writer's idea and its development to the stage where you can say that it is your idea rather than that of the original author. However, as far as acknowledging sources is concerned, the simple rule is, **if in doubt, source it out**. Never leave yourself open to the charge of plagiarism — passing off other people's ideas as your own. It's the academic equivalent of fraud and is treated as such by universities and colleges. Avoid plagiarism like the plague!

A handful of students who plagiarise are simply cheats — copying another student's work or large chunks from a book or article they have stumbled across. However, much more common is the situation where a student has read widely and ended up with an essay draft that is simply a succession of lengthy quotes from a number of sources, interspersed with the odd original linking phrase or sentence. It doesn't look right and the temptation is either to pass off some of the direct quotes as original text or, almost as bad, to change the occasional word or the word order (e.g. 'modern society' becomes 'contemporary society' and 'social and economic issues' becomes 'economic and social issues'). A much more useful and honest approach is to **look at each quote and ask yourself if you can say the same thing more concisely and clearly**. You'll be surprised how often the answer is yes. Remember that the authors of your reference materials are usually tackling different questions from the one that you have been set, and, as I pointed out earlier, there are still lots of academics who won't use one short word when two long ones will do!

So far in this discussion about citations I have concentrated on how to acknowledge written material. Occasionally you may want to use some **visual material** — a table or diagram. If you want to include the complete table or diagram, photocopy it and glue it into the final version of your essay. (The lipstick-type glue sticks are handy.) As with a direct quote, the source of the table or diagram must be acknowledged by adding details about the author, year and page number. Often you are interested in only part of the original diagram or table. You therefore need to draw your own simplified version. You still acknowledge the original author but show that your diagram or table is not identical to the original by adding 'Based on . . .', followed by the usual details of author, year and page number (see Table 2.1).

In the Harvard system the textual references, or citations, refer readers to a **reference list** at the end of the essay. The information in the reference list allows readers to find the original books and articles, and to follow up a particular point. The following comments give details about how to draw up a reference list.

With a **book**, you usually need to give details about the author, year of publication, title, the name of the publisher and the place of publication. I have already discussed problems that might arise with the author's name and year of publication. The title is virtually always straightforward. For books other than first editions you should give the number of the edition after the title. Remember that you can find this information on the imprint page which follows the main title page at the front of the book. Bear in mind that many government documents (e.g. parliamentary papers and ABS reports) have a reference number in addition to their title. It is often very useful to the reader if you give these reference numbers. The name of the publishers is often prominently displayed on the inside title page. If it is not there you can find it on the following imprint page which lists all the publishing details. Cut back full company titles to the basic name (e.g. Edward Arnold (Publishers) Ltd is listed simply as Edward Arnold). Place of publication refers to the city in which the publishers have their offices. You should find the city on the title or imprint page. Many publishers have offices in several cities, all of which may be listed. Find out which office is responsible for publishing this particular book — usually it's the first place on the list.

When you reference a **journal article** you need to give details of the author, year, title of the article, title of the journal, edition of the journal (volume, number and month) and the page numbers. Notice that neither the place of publication nor the publishers are needed. Usually you can easily find all the required details in the journal. Not all journals use a volume, number and month system for labelling each edition. Obviously, you must give whatever details are provided.

There is nothing worse than having a first-class quotation but not being able to recall exactly where you found it. (I speak from bitter experience!) You can waste a lot of valuable time tracking down the original book or article a second time. Recall my earlier advice to buy a pack of 127 mm × 76 mm (or 5" × 3") **catalogue cards** and to transfer onto a card all the necessary publishing details for each book or article you are likely to use (see Figure 2.7). Write the author's name at the top. (Capital letters help to minimise errors.) Cards are particularly useful as the reference list needs to be in alphabetical order by author's surname. You can easily arrange the cards so that they are in the right sequence when you come to type up the reference list. Under the heading 'References' include only the books and articles you have cited in the essay. If you find that there are other sources you haven't used yourself but are still relevant to the essay topic, you should list them separately under the heading 'Bibliography'.

Figure 3.7 gives details of the format used in the *Style Manual* (1988) for each of the most commonly occurring types of source

1. Books with one author
   Author, A.N. Year, <u>Book Title</u>, edition number (unless first), Publisher, Place.
   e.g.
   Bailey, R.F. 1984, <u>A Survival Kit for Writing English</u>, 2nd edn, Longman
      Cheshire, Melbourne.

2. Books with two or more authors
   Author, A.N. & Other, A.N. Year, <u>Book Title</u>, edition number (unless first),
      Publisher, Place.
   e.g.
   Bate, D. & Sharpe, P. 1990, <u>Student Writer's Handbook</u>, HBJ, Marrickville.

3. Articles
   Author, A.N. Year, 'Article title', <u>Journal Title</u>, volume, number, Month/
      Season, pages.
   e.g.
   Selvin, H.C. & Wilson, E.K. 1984, 'On sharpening sociologists' prose',
      <u>Sociological Quarterly</u>, vol. 25, no. 2, Spring, pp. 205–222.

4. Chapter in an edited book
   Author, A.N. Year, 'Chapter title', in <u>Book Title</u>, edition number (unless first),
      ed. A.N. Editor, Publisher, Place.
   e.g.
   Kaplan, H.B. 1989, 'Health, disease, and the social structure', in <u>Handbook
      of Medical Sociology</u>, 4th edn, eds H.E. Freeman & S. Levine, Prentice
      Hall, Englewood Cliffs (NJ).

5. Official report
   Official Group Year, <u>Report Title</u>, Reference number, Publisher, Place.
   e.g.
   Australian Bureau of Statistics 1990, <u>Catalogue of Publications and
      Products</u>, Cat. no. 1101.0, ABS, Canberra.

6. Anonymous book
   <u>Book Title</u> Year, edition number (unless the first), Publisher, Place.
   e.g.
   <u>Style Manual for Authors, Editors and Printers</u> 1988, 4th edn, AGPS,
      Canberra.

7. Anonymous article
   'Article title' Year, <u>Journal Title</u>, volume, number, date, pages.
   e.g.
   'The modern Adam Smith' 1990, <u>Economist</u>, vol. 316, no. 7663, 14 July,
      pp. 17–20.

8. Indirect quote (a quotation of a quotation)
   (Details of original source) quoted in (details of your source, including
      the number of the page where you found the quote).
   e.g.
   Hofstadter, D. 1982, '"Default assumptions" and their effects on writing
      and thinking', <u>Scientific American</u>, vol. 247, no. 5, pp. 14–21, quoted in
      Betts, K. & Seitz, A. 1986, <u>Writing Essays in the Social Sciences</u>, Nelson
      Wadsworth, Melbourne, p. 78.

Figure 3.7   Format for entries in a reference list using the Australian
government's version of the Harvard system.

material. I also use this format in my reference list, which you will find near the end of this book. However, recall that there are several versions of the Harvard system. For example, Figure 3.8 shows the standard format for entries in a psychology reference list, based on the instructions given in the *Publication Manual of the American Psychological Association* (1983).

Many of the general points made in the discussion of the Harvard system also apply to the **note system of referencing**. Therefore, I'll concentrate on the details of how to refer readers to the footnotes or endnotes, and how to present information in the notes about the books and articles you quote. Once again there are several versions of this system of acknowledging and referencing sources. If you're given a style sheet by a course lecturer, make sure that you follow it closely. If no specific instructions are given, use the following format, which is taken from the third and fourth editions of the Australian Government Publishing Service's *Style Manual* (1978, 1988).

Although special symbols (e.g. *, †, ‡) are traditionally used to refer to footnotes, it's more straightforward to **number each note**. Wherever possible, place each reference number at the end of a sentence and set it slightly above the general level of the line. Endnotes have to be numbered consecutively throughout the essay. Footnotes can either be numbered in the same way as endnotes, or you can start at '1' on each page. The second method is simpler if you end up adding or deleting notes as the amount of renumbering you need to do will be limited to any subsequent notes on the same page.

Use a **footnote format** similar to that shown at the bottom of this page. Footnotes are usually separated from the main text by a ruled line extending no more than 4 or 5 centimetres from the left margin. Use single line spacing (or, if possible, a smaller type size) for footnotes. Always bear in mind that the 'first reference to a work must provide all the information necessary to enable the reader to locate the work'.[1] The way the information is ordered in the footnote is shown in Figure 3.9. If you refer to the same source more than once, the second and subsequent references 'need not be as elaborate as the first'.[2] You have to include only the author's surname, or the main part of the title if it is an anonymous work,

---

1 *Style Manual for Authors, Editors and Printers*, 4th edn, Australian Government Publishing Service, Canberra, 1988, p. 151.
2 *Style Manual*, p. 151.

1. Books with one author
   Author, A. N. (Year). <u>Book title</u> (edition number (unless first)).
      Place: Publisher.
   e.g.
   Bailey, R. F. (1984). <u>A survival kit for writing English</u> (2nd ed.).
      Melbourne: Longman Cheshire.

2. Books with two or more authors
   Author, A. N., & Other, A. N. (Year). <u>Book title</u> (edition number (unless first)).
      Place: Publisher.
   e.g.
   Bate, D., & Sharpe, P. (1990). <u>Student writer's handbook</u>. Marrickville,
      NSW: HBJ.

3. Articles
   Author, A. N. (Year). Article title. <u>Journal Title</u>, <u>volume</u> (number), pages.
   e.g.
   Selvin, H. C., & Wilson, E. K. (1984). On sharpening sociologists' prose.
      <u>Sociological Quarterly</u>, <u>25</u> (2), 205–222.

4. Chapter in an edited book
   Author, A. N. (Year). Chapter title. In A. N. Editor (Ed.), <u>Book title</u> (edition number
      (unless first)) (pages). Place: Publisher.
   e.g.
   Kaplan, H. B. (1989). Health, disease, and the social structure. In H. E. Freeman
      & S. Levine (Eds.), <u>Handbook of medical sociology</u> (4th ed.) (pp. 46-68).
      Englewood Cliffs, NJ: Prentice Hall.

5. Official report
   Official Group. (Year). <u>Report title</u> (Reference number). Place: Publisher.
   e.g.
   Australian Bureau of Statistics. (1990). <u>Catalogue of publications and
      products</u> (Cat. no. 1101.0). Canberra: ABS.

6. Anonymous book
   <u>Book title</u> (edition number (unless first)). (Year). Place: Publisher.
   e.g.
   <u>Style manual for authors, editors and printers</u> (4th ed.). (1988). Canberra: AGPS.

7. Anonymous article in magazine
   Article title. (Year, Month, Day). <u>Magazine Title</u>, pages.
   e.g.
   The modern Adam Smith. (1990, July 14). <u>Economist</u>, pp. 17–20.

8. Indirect quote (a quotation of a quotation)
   Give details only of *your* source in the reference list. In the body of the essay
      use the format of the following example: 'According to Hofstadter (cited
      in Betts & Seitz, 1986, p. 78) . . .'

Figure 3.8   Format for entries in a reference list using the American
Psychological Association's version of the Harvard system

1. Books with one author
   A.N. Author, <u>Book Title</u>, edition number (unless first), Publisher, Place, Year.
   e.g.
   R.F. Bailey, <u>A Survival Kit for Writing English</u>, 2nd edn, Longman Cheshire, Melbourne, 1984.

2. Books with two or more authors
   A.N. Author & A.N. Other, <u>Book Title</u>, edition number (unless first), Publisher, Place, Year.
   e.g.
   D. Bate & P. Sharpe, <u>Student Writer's Handbook</u>, HBJ, Marrickville, 1990.

3. Articles
   A.N. Author, 'Article title', <u>Journal Title</u>, volume, number, Month/Season, pages.
   e.g.
   H.C. Selvin & E.K. Wilson, 'On sharpening sociologists' prose', <u>Sociological Quarterly</u>, vol. 25, no. 2, Spring, 1984, pp. 205–222.

4. Chapter in an edited book
   A.N. Author, 'Chapter title', in <u>Book Title</u>, edition number (unless first), ed. A.N. Editor, Publisher, Place, Year.
   e.g.
   H.B. Kaplan, 'Health, disease, and the social structure', in <u>Handbook of Medical Sociology</u>, 4th edn, eds H.E. Freeman & S. Levine, Prentice Hall, Englewood Cliffs (NJ), 1989.

5. Official report
   Official Group, <u>Report Title</u>, Reference number, Publisher, Place, Year.
   e.g.
   Australian Bureau of Statistics, <u>Catalogue of Publications and Products</u>, Cat. no. 1101.0, ABS, Canberra, 1990.

6. Anonymous book
   <u>Book Title</u>, edition number (unless the first), Publisher, Place, Year.
   e.g.
   <u>Style Manual for Authors, Editors and Printers</u>, 4th edn, AGPS, Canberra, 1988.

7. Anonymous article
   'Article title', <u>Journal Title</u>, volume, number, date, pages.
   e.g.
   'The modern Adam Smith', <u>Economist</u>, vol. 316, no. 7663, 14 July 1990, pp. 17–20.

8. Indirect quote (a quotation of a quotation)
   (Details of original source) quoted in (details of your source, including the number of the page where you found the quote).
   e.g.
   D. Hofstadter, '"Default assumptions" and their effects on writing and thinking', <u>Scientific American</u>, 247, 5, 1982, pp. 14–21, quoted in K. Betts & A. Seitz, <u>Writing Essays in the Social Sciences</u>, Nelson Wadsworth, Melbourne, 1986, p. 78.

Figure 3.9   Format for first entries using the Australian government's version of the note system

and the number of the page from which the quote is taken. Some people prefer always to give the book or article title as well as the author's name (e.g. Burdess, *Handbook of Student Skills*, p. 69). You *have* to give this extra information if you cite more than one work by the same author — if you don't, your reader won't be able to tell which book or article you're referring to.

You may come across notes that use the **Latin abbreviations** 'ibid.' (short for *ibidem*) and 'op. cit.' (short for *opere citato*). The abbreviation ibid. is used if two or more successive notes refer to the same source. For example, if I was using ibid., my second footnote would be 'ibid., p. 151'. This is because the second footnote refers to the same source as the previous footnote. The abbreviation op. cit. is used to refer back to an earlier note, though not the one immediately before. For example, if the first note refers to Smith, the second to Jones and the third to page 66 of the same article by Smith quoted earlier, then the third note would read 'op. cit., Smith, p. 66'. As you've probably gathered while reading through this paragraph, the simplest method is to forget about Latin abbreviations in your own writing! However, you need to know about them because you are likely to come across them in your reading.

Although an alphabetical **reference list** is optional in the footnote and endnote systems, I would recommend that you always add one in your assignments because a reference list can be very helpful for a marker. For example, if I've just read your essay I may want to check on the breadth of material used, or whether you referred to a particularly important reference. Bear in mind that markers' short-term memories often get rather hazy after marking several dozen papers, all answering the same question! The format of the entries in the reference list is only slightly different from that used in the first footnotes or endnotes for each citation. The main difference is that the author's surname is placed first in the reference list (e.g. Burdess, N.) whereas the first name or initials go first in a footnote or endnote entry.

Essay layout

Having discussed structure and style, I'll now turn my attention to the layout of the essay. This final, simple section is an important one. Even the most brilliant ideas seem better when presented well — and if the ideas are not so brilliant, top quality presentation is even more important! Many comments repeat earlier advice.

Recall my earlier exhortations to use a word processor or, failing that, a typewriter. **Typeface** helps you to read your paper as objectively as possible and thus identify problems more easily. Typeface also helps your lecturers to mark your papers as objectively as possible. Don't continue to use a typewriter ribbon that should have been replaced when the Beatles were performing! A new ribbon is money well spent. If you use your college or university computing facilities you will soon discover that the printers are often the weakest link in the whole system. Most places have several printers offering different standards of printing. Avoid using the relatively high quality printers until running off the final copy of your essay. The less unnecessary use these printers have the less likely they are to break down in the middle of your job.

Never cramp your work. Single-spaced text with narrow margins, typed on both sides of a sheet of paper will not endear you to your marker. It is difficult to read the text and it is impossible to find space to make written comments. Use double line spacing. Provide generous margins — about 4 centimetres on an A4 sheet. If you use a typewriter, rule these margins with a thick black crayon onto a blank page. Use it as a backing sheet each time you put a fresh page into the typewriter when typing your final copy. You will be able to see the ruled lines and use them to make sure that you always have the same margins. If you're using a printer attached to a computer, make sure that you know the instructions for setting up the margins.

Each page needs numbering — usually at the top right, or in the middle at the bottom. The position you choose can be marked onto the backing sheet. You can then always type the page number in the same spot. If using a printer, you will need to find the appropriate command for positioning the page numbers.

Your word processing package and printer may give you the choice of a **right-hand margin** that is justified or unjustified. With a justified right margin each line is made exactly the same length, usually by varying the width of the spaces between words. With an unjustified margin there are slight variations in line length depending on the words on each line. Experiment with each format to see which you prefer. I find it marginally easier to read text when there is the same single spacing between words — that is, when there is an unjustified right-hand margin.

I have already discussed the **format of the headings**. Recall my suggestion to have no more than two levels of heading, and to keep them as simple as possible. (Red typeface with green underlining is a definite no-no!) Use upper case for the major headings, and lower case for minor headings. Bold typeface looks better than underlining. You can do this with a typewriter by typing over each word in the heading two or three times. With a word processor, you will need to find the **bold** printing instruction. Numbering your headings can help emphasise the sequence of major and minor sections (see Figure 3.6). A heading should be positioned closer to the text beneath it (and to which it refers) than to the text above it. Thus, leave a blank line before the heading and start the following text on the line immediately after the heading.

Always leave the reader in no doubt about the **start of a new paragraph**. Indent the first word of each paragraph — that is, leave three or four empty character spaces between it and the usual left-hand margin. The only time when indenting is not necessary is at the start of a paragraph that comes immediately after a heading. You can emphasise your paragraph structure even more by adding a blank line between paragraphs.

Lengthy quotes should be indented by five character spaces from the left-hand margin, though the normal right-hand margin can still be used.

Supply a **title page**, complete with the full essay question, your name, unit, date, and the title (Prof, Dr, Ms, etc.) and name of your lecturer. Make triply sure that you spell the name of your lecturer correctly! In addition, you may be required to add a standard face-sheet provided by your department. If so, keep a few spare copies at home. If you use a printer with a continuous paper feeder, make sure you strip off the perforated edges and separate the pages. Check that all the pages are in numerical order and that none are upside down! The simplest way of securing the sheaf of papers is with a single staple in the top left-hand corner. A lecturer with over one hundred papers to mark prefers to start reading each paper with as little fuss as possible. Using a folder is not appreciated by your marker if it means that the essay has to be taken out to be read, and replaced after reading. (Placing each page in its own plastic sleeve is a definite no-no!)

Essays do sometimes go astray and, to say the least, it's rather galling to have to type out a second top copy from your final draft. Thus, if you're typing your essay it's a good idea to take a photocopy before handing it in. A carbon copy is cheaper but it may be rather faint if you use a backing sheet to show the typing margins. If you are using a word processor, make sure you never erase the text file before your essay has been marked and returned. Ideally, you should hang on to all your files for as long as possible — you never know when they might come in handy.

It's important, of course, to **keep to deadlines**. They are there to ensure that all students have the same time available for writing the essay. They also help staff to mark and return papers as effectively and efficiently as possible. If there are exceptional circumstances which mean you can't meet an essay deadline, you should see the appropriate person as soon as possible about an extension. 'Exceptional circumstances' are usually strictly defined. If you have been ill you may need to provide a medical certificate. If there has been a family crisis — particularly if it has gone on for some time and you are behind with more than one assignment — it is easier to explain the situation once to a student counsellor, and ask him or her to give you written support for a request for an extension. As I pointed out in Chapter 1, you should find out the procedure at the start of the year so that if exceptional circumstances do arise you know exactly what to do.

Pressure of work, problems with library books and the failure of some part of the computer system for a few hours arc usually not accepted as circumstances warranting an extension. You are expected to plan your time to take these perennial problems into account. **Aim to have your final copy ready at least 24 hours before the deadline.** This gives you some room for manoeuvre. If you have to rush the preparation of the final copy of the essay, you are likely to find that the layout of the paper does not do full justice to the time and effort you have spent working on the structure and style.

Finally, when your essay is returned, don't simply look at the mark, express suitable comments of delight or disappointment, and consign the paper to the bottom drawer. **Look carefully at all the comments.** They will have taken considerable time to write and are there to help you make your next essay a better one. This feedback is thus important. If you can't read or understand the marker's comments ask for clarification. Similarly, if your 2000 word *magnum opus* comes back to you with a tick (or even several ticks), a one-word commentary ('Good', 'Satisfactory', etc.) and a mark, you should ask the marker for more feedback. For example, if your mark is 62%, you need to know about the problems, omissions and so on that account for the remaining 38%.

Further reading

More advice about developing your writing skills can be found in the following books:

Betts, K. & Seitz, A. 1986, *Writing Essays in the Social Sciences*, Nelson Wadsworth, Melbourne.

Cuba, L.J. 1987, *A Short Guide to Writing about Social Science*, Scott Foresman, Glenview (Illinois).

Dunleavy, P. 1986, *Studying for a Degree in the Humanities and Social Sciences*, Macmillan, Basingstoke.

Taylor, G. 1989, *The Student's Writing Guide for the Arts and Social Sciences*, Cambridge University Press, Cambridge.

The following book is mainly for graduate students, but it is written with such clarity and verve that any student (and almost any lecturer) would benefit from reading it:

Becker, H.S. 1986, *Writing for Social Scientists: How to Start and Finish Your Thesis, Book or Article*, University of Chicago Press, Chicago.

Appendix 1000 commonly misspelled words

A dictionary is made up of three types of words:

1. those that you don't know and thus don't use;
2. those that you know and can spell; and
3. those that you know, but aren't sure of the spelling.

There's probably only a few hundred words in this last group. Hopefully, most of them are included in the following 1000 words. I suggest that you photocopy the list and put it at the front of your working file. You'll find it very useful.

There are many words which are spelled differently in British English and American English (e.g. centre (UK) and center (USA), defence (UK) and defense (USA)). Traditionally, Australian English has adopted the British version. However, you will frequently come across American English spellings, as much of the social science literature originates in the USA. More generally, the trend is towards greater acceptance of American spellings. For example, 'program' (USA) is now preferred to 'programme' (UK); you are more likely to see reference to computer 'disks' (USA) than 'discs' (UK); and some newspapers now use the American 'or' ending instead of the British 'our' ending (e.g. color, flavor, vigor).

Both British and American forms are included in the *Macquarie Dictionary: Second Revision* (1987), the British form being defined as the commonest Australian spelling, and the US spelling as a variant spelling. I have not filled up the list with words that suffer from having both British and American spellings. It seems to me that you have better things to do than check whether the preferred Australian spelling is, for example, 'skilful' or 'skillful'. In a couple of instances (analyse/analyze, manoeuvre/maneuver) where both forms are sometimes misspelled, I have included both. Occasionally, a single spelling is used, even though the word is derived from one which does have different British and American spellings (e.g. 'honorary' is the agreed spelling, even though the word from which it is derived is spelled 'honor' in American English and 'honour' in British English). In these cases, I have included the one common spelling.

a lot
abbreviate
abbreviation
abolition
absence
abundance
abundant
academic
academically
academy
accede
access
accessibility
accessible
accident
accidentally
acclaim
acclamation
accommodate
accommodation
achievable
achieve
achievement
achiever
achieving
acquaintance
acquiesce
acquire
acquit
acquitted
adamant
adapt
adaptation
address
adequate
adherence
adherent
adjective
administer
administration
administrative

advertisement
aerial
aggravate
aggravation
aggression
aggressive
aggressor
alcohol
alcoholic
alienate
alienation
align
alignment
allegation
allege
allegedly
allegiance
alleviate
allocate
allocation
allot
allotted
already
altogether
amend
amendment
among
amongst
amount
analogy
analyse, *or*
analyze (US)
analysis
analytical
analytically
ancillary
anecdotal
anecdote
annihilate
annoy
anonymity

anonymous
Antarctic
anxious
appal
appalled
appalling
apparatus
apparent
apparently
appeal
appealed
appealing
appear
appearance
appropriate
appropriately
archaeologist, *or*
archeologist
archaeology, *or*
archeology
Arctic
arguable
arguably
argue
argument
article
as well
ascertain
assistance
associate
association
assume
assuming
assumption
assurance
assured
assuring
asymmetrical
asymmetry
atrocious
atrociously

attach
attachment
attendance
attendant
authoritarian
authoritatively
authority
auxiliary
availability
available
avoid
awkward
awkwardly

bankruptcy
basically
beautiful
become
beggar
beginning
believable
believe
beneficial
benefit
benefited
benefiting
blatant
blatantly
boisterous
boundary
bourgeois
bourgeoisie
Britain
buoyant
bureau
bureaucracy
bureaucratic
business

calculable
calendar

campaign
cancel
cancellation
canister
capital
capitalism
capitalist
career
caricature
catalogue
catastrophe
catastrophic
categorise, *or*
categorize
category
ceiling
cemetery
censor
census
central
centralise, *or*
centralize
centrality
century
ceremonial
ceremony
challenge
changeable
character
chargeable
charisma
charismatic
chauvinism
chauvinist
chauvinistic
chief
choice
Christian
circuit
cognition
cognitive

coincide
coincidence
collaborate
collaborator
colleague
college
collegiate
collision
colonel
commemorate
commemoration
commend
commendable
commission
commit
commitment
committed
committee
commodity
comparative
comparatively
comparison
compatibility
compatible
compel
compelled
compensate
compensation
competent
competently
competitive
competitively
comprehend
comprehensible
comprehensive
computer
conceit
concept
conceivable
conceive
concentrate

concentric
concept
condemn
condemnation
condemned
connotation
conquer
conquered
conscience
conscientious
conscious
consciousness
consensus
considered
consistent
consolidate
constant
construe
construed
contemporary
contempt
contemptible
contradict
contradictory
contributor
control
controllable
controlled
controller
controversial
controversy
conurbation
convenience
convenient
corporal
correspondence
corroborate
corroboration
counterfeit
courteous
create

creation
criticise, *or*
criticize
criticism
cue
curriculum
cynic
cynicism

debatable
deceit
deceivable
deceive
decision
decrepit
deductible
defendant
defensible
defensive
definite
definitely
definition
degradation
delegate
delegation
deliberate
deliberately
demonstrate
demonstration
denigrate
denigration
deplete
depletion
description
desirable
despair
desperate
desperately
despite
deter
deteriorate

determine
deterred
deterrent
detriment
detrimental
devastate
develop
development
develops
deviance
deviancy
deviant
diaphragm
dichotomy
dietary
difference
different
dilapidate
dilapidation
dilemma
disappear
disappeared
disaster
disastrous
discernible
disciple
disciplinary
discipline
discretion
discriminate
discrimination
disintegrate
disintegration
dispensable
disprove
dissident
dissimilar
dissipate
distinct
division
doctor

dominance
dominant
dormant
dramatically
drunkenness
duly

earned
economically
ecstasy
eight
eighth
eliminate
elimination
embarrass
embarrassing
embarrassment
embryo
embryos
emigrate
emigration
eminent
eminently
emperor
emphasis
emphasise
encompass
encroach
encroaches
enforceable
enormous
environment
equilibrium
equip
equipment
equipped
equipping
erupt
eruption
essential
euthanasia

eventually
evolutionary
exaggerate
exaggeration
excel
excellence
excellent
excelling
excitable
excite
excitement
exemplify
exhilarate
exhilarating
exist
existence
existent
exorbitant
explain
explainable
explanation
explanatory
extraordinary

facilitate
facility
facsimile
familiar
fascinate
feasibility
feasible
February
feminine
femininity
feud
field
finally
finite
flamboyant
flexibility
flexible

fluorescent
forcible
forecast
foreign
foreigner
foresee
foreshadow
forest
forewarn
foreword
forfeit
fortunate
fortunately
fourteen
fourth (4th)
friend
further

gadgetry
galloped
gauge
ghettos
goddess
government
governor
graffiti
grammar
grief
grieve
guarantee
guaranteed
guard
guardian
guerilla
guidance

haphazard
harass
harassment
harmful
hazard

hazardous
helpful
helpfulness
hereditary
heterogeneous
hierarchical
hierarchy
hindrance
homogeneous
honorary
humorous
hygiene

identical
ideology
idiosyncrasy
immediate
immediately
immigrant
immigration
imminent
impenetrable
imperative
in fact
in turn
inadvertent
incidentally
incompatible
incurred
indefinite
indefinitely
independence
independent
indispensable
indistinct
indubitably
inevitable
infallible
infinite
infinitely
information

innate
innocuous
innuendoes
inoculate
insistence
insistent
insoluble
integrate
intensely
interest
interfere
interpret
interpreter
interpreting
interrupt
interruption
intervene
intricacy
investigator
involvement
irreconcilable
irreparable
irresistible
irreverent
irreversible
irrigation
irritation
Israel

jealous
jeopardise, *or*
jeopardize
jeopardy
journal
jubilant
jurisdiction

keenness
kilogram
knowledge
knowledgeable

known

laboratory
laid (not layed)
lawsuit
legitimacy
legitimate
leisure
leisurely
liaison
library
lieutenant
likeable
likelihood
literature
livable
livelihood
loneliness
lonely

machinery
maintain
maintenance
manageable
manoeuvre, *or*
maneuver (US)
marihuana, *or*
marijuana
mathematics
meant
Mediterranean
merely
message
messenger
meteorological
meteorology
microfiche
milieu
mimic
mimicked
mimicry

miniature
ministry
miracle
miscellaneous
mischievous
misconstrue
monitor
monotonous
monotony
motivate
motivation
murmuring
mystifying

naive
natural
naturally
necessarily
necessary
negative
negotiable
negotiate
nonsense
nostalgia
notable
notably
noticeable
nuclear
nuisance
nurture

obedience
obedient
objector
obsolescence
obsolescent
obsolete
obstacle
occasion
occasionally
occur

occurred
occurrence
occurring
offered
offering
official
officially
officious
omission
omit
omitted
opening
openness
opponent
opportunity
optimistic
ordinarily
ordinary
origin
original
outspokenness
override
overriding
overrule
overruling

paid (not
  payed)
palliative
paradigm
paraffin
parallel
paranoid
parliament
parliamentary
particular
particularly
patriarchal
patriarchy
peculiar
people

perceive
perceptible
performance
perhaps
permanent
permanently
permissible
perseverance
persistence
persistent
personnel
persuade
persuasive
pesticide
phenomena
phenomenon
Philippines
physical
physically
physician
piece
pinnacle
playwright
poison
poisonous
polar
policy
political
politician
pollution
positive
possess
possessive
practitioner
precede
precedence
precedent
precious
prefer
preference
preferred

preferring
prejudice
prejudicial
preparation
prepare
presence
prestigious
prevail
prevalence
prevalent
primary
privilege
privileged
procedure
proceed
process
procession
processor
profession
professional
proffer
proffered
proficiency
proficient
programmed
programming
proletariat
prominent
pronunciation
propeller
proponent
proprietor
proprietorial
prosperous
prove
psychiatric
psychiatrist
psychiatry
psychological
psychologist
psychology

publicly
punctuation
pursue

queried
query
querying
questionnaire
queue
queuing
quotient

racism
racist
really
recede
receive
recession
receipt
reciprocal
recommend
recommendation
reconcilable
refer
referee
reference
referral
referred
referring
refrigerator
regard
regarding
register
registered
registering
regrettable
regrettably
regular
regularly
reign
relative

relatively
relegate
relevance
relevant
religious
religiously
rely
reminiscence
reminiscent
repentant
repetition
repetitive
repetitively
research
researcher
resemblance
reservoir
resistant
resource
respectability
respondent
response
responsibility
restaurant
resuscitate
reticent
reveal
reversible
rhetorical
rhyme
rhythm
rigid
rigorous

sacrilege
sacrilegious
saleable
satellite
scenery
seaboard
secondary

secrecy
secretary
segregate
seize
sense
sensible
sensitive
separate
separately
sergeant
sheriff
sieve
signature
significance
significant
similar
similarly
sincere
sincerely
sizeable
sociable
solely
solicitor
souvenir
sovereignty
spacious
spaciousness
spatial
spatially
special
specially
spectacular
strategy
submit
subservience
subservient
substantial
substantially
subtle
subtly
success

successful
successfully
succinct
succinctly
suddenness
suffice
sufficient
suggest
summarise
summary
superb
superintendent
supersede
superseding
supplement
support
suppress
suppression
supremacy
survey
survive
survivor
susceptibility
susceptible
suspicious
suspiciously
sustain
sustenance
symmetrical
symmetrically
symmetry

taboo
taboos
taxied
taxiing, *or*
taxying
technical
technique
temperature
temporarily

temporary
tenant
tendency
tertiary
thorough
thought
threatened
through
throughout
tight
tobacco
tongue
totalitarian
transfer
transferable
transferred
transferring
transience
transient
triple
truly
twelfth
tyranny

unbelievable
underlie
undoubtedly
unfortunate
unfortunately
unmistakably
unnecessary
unparalleled
unrepentant
unsociable
until
up to
usage
useful
useless
utilise, *or*
utilize

vacuum	vicious	voluntarily	woollen
valuable	viciously	voluntary	worshipper
variable	view	vulnerable	worshipping
variance	vigorous		writing
vegetable	violence	warrant	written
vehicle	violent	Wednesday	
vengeance	virtual	whether	yacht
versatile	virtually	which	yield
vertical	volcano	wholly	
vertically	volcanoes	withdrawal	zeros

References

Abercrombie, N., Hill, S. & Turner, B.S. 1984, *The Penguin Dictionary of Sociology,* Penguin, Harmondsworth.

Adams, G.R. & Schvaneveldt, J.D. 1985, *Understanding Research Methods,* Longman, New York.

Australia, Parliament 1987, *Australian Bureau of Statistics: Annual Report 1986–87,* Parl. Paper 222, Canberra.

Australia, Parliament 1989, *Australian Bureau of Statistics: Annual Report 1988–89,* Parl. Paper 256, Canberra.

Australian Bureau of Statistics 1986a, *How Australia Takes a Census,* Cat. no. 2176.0, ABS, Canberra.

Australian Bureau of Statistics 1986b, *1986 Census Dictionary,* Cat. no. 2174.0, ABS, Canberra.

Australian Bureau of Statistics 1987, *Australian Standard Geographical Classification Geographic Code List,* Cat. no. 2188.0, ABS, Canberra.

Australian Bureau of Statistics 1990a, *Catalogue of Publications and Products,* Cat. no. 1101.0, ABS, Canberra.

Australian Bureau of Statistics 1990b, *Labour Mobility in Australia During the Year Ending February 1989,* Cat. no. 6209.0, ABS, Canberra.

Australian National Bibliography 1988 1989, National Library of Australia, Canberra.

Bailey, R.F. 1984, *A Survival Kit for Writing English,* 2nd edn, Longman Cheshire, Melbourne.

Bandt, P.L., Meara, N.M. & Schmidt, L.D. 1974, *A Time to Learn,* Holt Rinehart and Winston, New York.

Bart, P. & Frankel, L. 1986, *The Student Sociologist's Handbook,* 4th edn, Random House, New York.

174

Bate D. & Sharpe P. 1990, *Student Writer's Handbook*, HBJ, Marrickville.

Bates, E. & Linder-Pelz, S. 1990, *Health Care Issues*, 2nd edn, Allen & Unwin, North Sydney.

Berry, R. 1986, *How to Write a Research Paper*, Pergamon, Oxford.

Betts, K. & Seitz, A. 1986, *Writing Essays in the Social Sciences*, Nelson Wadsworth, Melbourne.

Bryson, B. 1987, *The Penguin Dictionary of Troublesome Words*, 2nd edn, Penguin, London.

Burdess, N. 1986a, 'Participation in local planning: a practical proposition', *Australian Local Planner*, December, pp. 36–9.

Burdess, N. 1986b, 'Social change in rural Britain: a review', *Regional Journal of Social Issues*, no. 19, December, pp. 18–30.

Cooperative Action by Victorian Academic Libraries 1990, *Reciprocal Borrowing at Your Tertiary Library*, CAVAL, Camberwell.

Cuba, L.J. 1987, *A Short Guide to Writing about Social Science*, Scott Foresman, Glenview (Illinois).

Dewey Decimal Classification and Relative Index, Volume 2, Schedules 000-599 1989, 20th edn, ed. J.P. Comaromi, Forest Press, Albany (NY).

Dixon, J. 1988, *How to be a Successful Student without Quitting the Human Race!*, Penguin, Ringwood (Victoria).

Dunleavy, P. 1986, *Studying for a Degree in the Humanities and Social Sciences*, Macmillan, Basingstoke.

Fogarty, M.F. 1987, 'Student teacher stress in field studies', *Unicorn*, vol. 13, no. 1, February, pp. 51–3.

Fussell, P. 1989, *Wartime*, Oxford University Press, New York.

Gibbs, G., Habeshaw, S. & Habeshaw, T. 1987, *53 Interesting Things to Do in Your Lectures*, 2nd edn, Technical and Educational Services, Bristol.

Guy, R.F., Edgely, C.E., Arafat, I. & Allen, D.E. 1987, *Social Research Methods: Puzzles and Solutions*, Allyn & Bacon, Boston.

Habeshaw, S., Habeshaw, T. & Gibbs, G. 1987, *53 Interesting Things to Do in Your Seminars and Tutorials*, 2nd edn, Technical and Educational Services, Bristol.

Harris, J.S. & Blake, R.H. 1976, *Technical Writing for Social Scientists*, Nelson Hall, Chicago.

Hastings, E. 1984, *How to Study at Tertiary Level*, Nelson, Melbourne.

Higbee, K.L. 1988, *Your Memory: How It Works and How To Improve It*, 2nd edn, Prentice Hall, Englewood Cliffs (New Jersey).

International Encyclopedia of the Social Sciences 1968, ed. D. Sills, Macmillan and Free Press, New York.

Johnson, P.B. 1988, 'Drinking-related beliefs of male college students', *Journal of Alcohol and Drug Education*, vol. 34, no. 1, pp. 17–22.

Kass, L.R. 1975, 'Regarding the end of medicine and the pursuit of health', *Public Interest*, vol. 40, Summer, pp. 11–42.

Kinnersly, P. 1974, *The Hazards of Work: How to Fight Them*, Pluto Press, London.

Lane, N.D. 1989, *Techniques for Student Research: A Practical Guide*, Longman Cheshire, Melbourne.

Macquarie Dictionary: Second Revision 1987, Macquarie Library, Macquarie University (Sydney).

Marshall L.A. & Rowland F. 1981, *A Guide to Learning Independently*, Longman Cheshire, Melbourne.

McEvedy M.R. & Jordan, M. 1986, *Succeeding at University and College*, Nelson, Melbourne.

McEvedy, M.R., Packham, G. & Smith, P. 1986, *Speaking in Academic Settings*, Nelson, Melbourne.

Orr, F. 1984, *How to Pass Exams*, Allen & Unwin, North Sydney.

Orr, F. 1988, *How to Succeed at Part-time Study*, Allen & Unwin, North Sydney.

Percy, D. 1983, *Study Tactics*, Macmillan, South Melbourne.

Publication Manual of the American Psychological Association 1983, 3rd edn, American Psychological Association, Washington DC.

Roget's Thesaurus of English Words and Phrases 1966 (1852), rev. R.A. Dutch, Penguin, Harmondsworth.

Scharf, D. with Hait, P. 1985, *Studying Smart: Time Management for College Students*, Barnes & Noble, New York.

Selvin, H.C. & Wilson, E.K. 1984a, 'On sharpening sociologists' prose', *Sociological Quarterly*, vol. 25, no. 2, Spring, pp. 205–22.

Selvin, H.C. & Wilson, E.K. 1984b, 'Cases in point', *Sociological Quarterly*, vol. 25, no. 3, Summer, pp. 417–27.

Social Science Encyclopedia 1985, eds A. Kruper & J. Kruper, Routledge Kegan Paul, London.

Style Manual for Authors, Editors and Printers 1978, 3rd edn, AGPS, Canberra.

Style Manual for Authors, Editors and Printers 1988, 4th edn, AGPS, Canberra.

Temple, M. 1978, *A Pocket Guide to Written English*, John Murray, London.

Verderber R.F. 1988, *The Challenge of Effective Speaking*, 7th edn, Wadsworth, Belmont (California).

Victorian Women's Consultative Council 1988, *Women in the Home: It Was Nice to be Asked*, rev. edn, VWCC, Melbourne.

Wade, J. 1990, *Superstudy: A New Age Guide*, Dellasta, Melbourne.

Whitehorn, J. 1989, *Women in the Home*, Women's Adviser's Office, Adelaide.

Williamson, S.T. 1947, 'How to write like a social scientist', *Saturday Review*, 4 Oct., p. 17, quoted in Harris, J.S. & Blake, R.H. 1976, *Technical Writing for Social Scientists*, Nelson Hall, Chicago, p. 7.

Index